Communication Skill Training & Long distance Real Estate Investing

Christopher Rothchester

© Copyright 2022 by Christopher Rothchester. All right reserved.

The work contained herein has been produced with the intent to provide relevant knowledge and information on the topic described in the title for entertainment purposes only. While the author has gone to every extent to furnish up to date and true information, no claims can be made as to its accuracy or validity as the author has made no claims to be an expert on this topic. Notwithstanding, the reader is asked to do their own research and consult any subject matter experts they deem necessary to ensure the quality and accuracy of the material presented herein.

This statement is legally binding as deemed by the Committee of Publishers Association and the American Bar Association for the territory of the United States. Other jurisdictions may apply their own legal statutes. Any reproduction, transmission or copying of this material contained in this work without the express written consent of the copyright holder shall be deemed as a copyright violation as per the current legislation in force on the date of publishing and subsequent time thereafter. All additional works derived from this material may be claimed by the holder of this copyright.

The data, depictions, events, descriptions and all other information forthwith are considered to be true, fair and accurate unless the work is expressly described as a work of fiction. Regardless of the nature of this work, the Publisher is exempt from any responsibility of actions taken by the reader in conjunction with this work. The Publisher acknowledges that the reader acts of their own accord and releases the author and Publisher of any responsibility for the observance of tips, advice, counsel, strategies and techniques that may be offered in this volume.

Table of Contents

Communication Skills Training 6

Introduction 7

Chapter 1: Communication Obstacles And How To Avoid 13

Chapter 2: Expressing Anger And Managing Conflicts 23

Chapter 3: Reading Faces And Predicting Behavior 33

Chapter 4: Giving And Receiving Feedback 42

Chapter 5: Building Rapport, Networking, And Creating A Unique .. 52

Chapter 6: The Foundations Of Communication, The Forms It 62

Chapter 7: The Biggest Mistakes People Make When 69

Chapter 8: How To Read People And Connect With Different 74

Chapter 9: The Invisible Barriers Against Effective 83

Chapter 10: Secrets To Becoming An Empathetic Listener And 93

Chapter 11: How To Form Your Message To Get Your Point 102

Chapter 12: The Art Of Conveying Your Thoughts And Feelings.... 110

Chapter 13: How To Give Useful Feedback Without Offending..... 123

Conclusion 135

Long Distance Real Estate Investing 140

Introduction 141

Chapter 1: Is Long-Distance Investing Risky? 145

Chapter 2: Making An A Team 162

Chapter 3: Using The Internet To Find Deals 185

Chapter 4: Keep Up To Date With The Market 207

Chapter 5: Structuring Your Deal 218

Chapter 6: Managing Property In Different Cities 231

Chapter 7: Types Of Investment Strategies For Long Distance 247

Chapter 8: Tips On How To Become A Successful Long-Distance .. 256

Conclusion 269

Communication Skills Training

How to Talk to Anyone at Any Time and Read People Like a Book

Christopher Rothchester

Introduction

Have you ever been in a public place, and when you needed to speak with someone nearby, you became nervous and couldn't find the right words? Have you ever been trying to read body language but found yourself confused by mixed signals? And have you ever wondered how some people could walk up to strangers and strike up a conversation like it's the most normal thing in the world?

It can sometimes feel like anyone can walk up to you and start a conversation. It's your job to learn how to talk nicely, don't let anyone step up to you and think that it's okay for them to start chatting away. This book will share tips for communicating well with others, from getting past your shyness to reading body language like an expert.

If you're shy, like many others, it will take a bit more than just reading this book. It will require new habits, so you can walk up to strangers and feel comfortable. If you're a person that doesn't like approaching others, then consider keeping an active journal or writing in a diary. This can help with your social skills and conversation skills at the same time. It's good to learn how to have a conversation and have it become more than just talking, so keep at it.

Now, don't be discouraged if you feel like this book won't work for you. It'll take some practice before being able to observe other people and be able to read their body language correctly. This social skill requires time, but it will also need time to apply the skills you learn.

Many people will understand that they're reading this and think, "I've already done this." or "It sounds easy." The first thing they do is go out in public and try their hand at acting naturally in a conversation with another person. It's not as easy as it sounds. First, you have to be able to communicate well with another person. But also, you have to take the time and listen to what the other person is saying. Each conversation is a learning experience, and you don't want to have that experience be something you leave with a bad taste in your mouth about yourself.

Communication can improve your life significantly and make things better for everyone around you. Take the time to try and improve your communication skills and see how it makes you feel. People around you will be happy that you're a kind, friendly person they can talk to at any time.

If you want to improve your social, communication, and conversation skills, then you should pay attention and use your social skills as much as possible. People who don't talk to others often won't get to practice their social skills much, so it's good for them to learn these things.

Communication isn't just about having a conversation with another person. It means making sure that your words reach their intended target meaning is clear and not at all confusing. It also is about reading body language. Someone can be talking to you without learning this skill, but you might not understand what they're saying. When reading body language, you mustn't make assumptions about that person. It's better for them if you let them tell you what's going on than to jump to conclusions.

Once you're able to make a conversation with someone, and it starts with you talking to them, it's even better. That person will feel more comfortable speaking with you, and you'll have the confidence to talk about things that come up for you. It suits your social skills because you've already made a friendly first impression.

Talking to someone is just like anything else. It takes practice to be good at it. But, if you put in the time and effort to research things, you'll be able to learn everything about it in no time. You may feel that it's too difficult for you to speak up and make your voice heard, but this is something that can be easily overcome by putting your thoughts into writing first. It's so much easier to express yourself in writing, and then you can go back and see what you wrote down. If you can make sense of what you said, it will be easy for you to say the same thing out loud.

It's easier for people to speak with others if they know the conversation will be about them. This is one of the essential things in any conversation. Everyone wants someone else to listen to what they have to say. We often can't get this from others because we don't even give them a chance. We don't have time for them or may not even like spending time with others. If you think about others and want them to listen to you, you must ensure they're getting something out of the conversation, too. Pay attention and find out what it is that they like. If they carry a camera, find out if they want to take pictures. If they have a phone, see if they like talking on it or playing games. You can learn so much about others by just paying attention.

Sometimes, people will do things to get attention from other people. One example is when someone makes a scene because someone doesn't talk with them or pay attention to what's happening around them. Another, perhaps more difficult to forgive, an example is someone who pretends not to find something funny or bothersome. Many people don't realize that some people use their body language to signal interest in others. This is why paying attention to how someone else communicates with you is essential.

You can learn so much when talking with others who are different from you. This can be done by asking them many questions about day-to-day life. It's also essential to ensure you're not being a pest when trying to learn about something from someone else. Just because they are willing to talk with you doesn't mean they want to speak with you all the time.

Remember this when approaching others to ask them questions. You don't need to be friends with everyone, and you don't want to be. It's okay to tell someone you aren't interested in being friends or don't want to talk with them because you feel like it's not a good time for you.

It can be challenging for shy people to speak with others. This isn't something that is overcome overnight but can be overcome if you're willing to invest the time and effort necessary. Once you realize how hard work learning social skills can be, you won't mind putting in the time and effort needed. Take the first step by listening to what people have to say instead of thinking about what you will say next. You'll learn so much by listening to what people say.

The conversation can be anything from small talk to deep and meaningful discussions. How you conduct the conversation and what you talk about is different, depending on your social, communication, and exchange skills. Whatever you choose to talk about, it's up to you to lead the conversation. This is something that takes time and practice. Once you learn how to have a conversation, don't be afraid of having a conversation with others. You have social skills if you've learned how to communicate with people!

An essential thing in a conversation is talking and listening. There are many forms of communication, but all of them are important. It's suitable for people who want to become better communicators; they should also work on their body language. If you don't like how someone is talking to you, you can always reject them and tell them how you feel. You never want to be forced into a conversation that makes you uncomfortable. The same thing goes for others as well. If someone talks to others in a way that makes them uncomfortable, it's okay if they reject the person telling them they don't want to talk with them. Communication is about mutual understanding's feelings and body language, so there shouldn't be any hard feelings afterward. Better communication skills make life easier, and people will like you more.

You don't need to know everything about everything. You can learn a lot by asking many questions and then taking note of the answers. Taking things in slowly is good for your brain and social skills. If you're unsure if you can answer any questions, there's no problem with asking them. Having a conversation with someone will always be successful if you learn to get it started first by listening to what they want to talk about and what they don't want. When talking with others, you must speak directly about whatever topic is discussed between you two. It's also important to remember that there are two sides to a conversation, so you can't forget about listening and talking.

Chapter 1: Communication Obstacles and How to Avoid Them

Communication can be the most frustrating and difficult thing in the world. It's one of those things that, no matter how confident you may be, can make you feel vulnerable. We know this is because everyone has different expectations on how a conversation "should" go- but what if we could change that? How? By using a simple technique that is often overlooked when it comes to communication. The right tone, body language, and how you say things are crucial aspects of speaking with others.

What's more, is that you can do this whether you're shy or outgoing; it doesn't matter. However, if you've ever seen someone with extroverted personality traits (those who are naturally outgoing), this technique may seem second nature to them. Great leaders are those who have mastered this skill.

Most will tell you to "be yourself" or "just relax." It may be just a simple thing to say but think about it. How often do you break out of your comfort zone and try something different? It's hard, right? But what if there was a technique that could help you do this?

The key to success is not trying to be someone else but communicating your genuine thoughts, feelings, and opinions. This can be scary and hard at first, but the more you practice, the easier it'll be.

Let's cover some common mistakes most often made when speaking with others. Most people find public speaking one of the scariest things they have to do. There's nothing worse than standing in front of a group of people, sweating, and your mind drawing a blank on what to say next. It's embarrassing and normal to feel this way if you're not confident in yourself or your abilities.

However, this is where the beauty of communication skills training comes in. You can learn how to speak with anyone anytime and read people like a book. It's not easy by any means, but there are some tips and tricks to get you started. Find an opportunity to practice daily with your partner, a work colleague, or family. Regardless of the situation you find yourself in, these tips will help you avoid common pitfalls.

The tone goes a long way when establishing rapport with others. Knowing how to talk assertively is crucial to adding value to others and getting your point across clearly and concisely. Start by using a soft, relaxed tone. This will allow you to speak in a way that those around you will be able to hear and understand. This can be aided by adopting slow breaths and standing with your feet planted firmly on the ground. It's easier for others to understand you when you're speaking clearly, which makes them more likely to listen and pay attention to what you're saying.

Try to avoid any sharp movements or abrupt hand gestures. Your body language can reflect your voice, so if you're speaking in an angry tone, with your arms crossed, or simply jutting out your jaw, they will draw the same assumptions. Take a deep breath, and think before you act. It's hard to do this in scenarios where someone has accused you of something terrible, but overreacting can worsen things.

Being genuine is essential when getting to know others. Don't be too aggressive or standoffish when meeting new people for the first time. A gentle gesture here or there should suffice, rather than saying something rude on purpose or being overly reserved. You may think being mean or harsh to your roommate, friends, or family will keep you from being hurt, but this is a childish way of thinking. People rarely remember the first impression of someone and whether you like it; things will get better over time.

Doing so shows that you're just as dedicated and determined about speaking to others as they are.
In a conversation, you should try to be the one to let the other person know that you're interested in them. This means learning to talk positively about what's happening in your head and life. The goal is for people around you to feel comfortable around you – make them feel welcome and loved by drawing out their best qualities. Never assume they're straight-out rude to you.

Being too aggressive or trying to dominate others makes them feel uncomfortable around you. When it comes down to it, we all want to be accepted and loved by others. No one wants to be disliked or feared, so being assertive is key to establishing trust when speaking with others.

If someone's not getting what you're saying, they may give up on the conversation altogether. It's your job as a leader and communicator to try and understand where they are coming from by accepting their perspective, even if it doesn't match their own. Ask questions instead of attempting to persuade or force your point of view onto them.

Try having an open mind and thinking about putting yourself in their shoes before speaking. This may be one of the hardest things to do, but it's also an excellent way to let go of controlling your emotions. It may be hard at first, but the more you practice, the better you'll get at expressing yourself in a manner that allows others to understand where you're coming from.

Another way to become more confident in your ability to speak with anyone is by practicing how you say things. How you say something can be just as important as what you're saying. You may be saying everything right but pronouncing them wrong. Saying something the wrong way may cause someone to misunderstand you or even make them feel upset.

The main thing is to keep in mind that no one can judge you for being a confident speaker. If anything, people will admire and take notice of your authenticity and character. Even if it's challenging to be yourself, you must realize you're already great at being yourself. How we communicate with others is just as important as the words that come out of our mouths; you can use these tips the next time you find yourself in a public situation. You don't have to feel nervous or intimidated when talking to people. You'll find yourself enjoying time with new people more and more. Dedicating yourself to personal growth is a great way to learn how to speak with anyone. Over time, you'll notice a significant difference in how much more comfortable you feel when socializing with others. This, in turn, will lead you to become more confident throughout the rest of your day; just remember that practice makes perfect.

If anything, these tips should allow you to be yourself and use your natural communication skills. The more you practice, the better you will become at it. Practice like your life depends on it. Follow these simple tips; then, you can become one of those people who can speak with anyone. You may not be able to give an eloquent speech, but you should be able to speak so others understand you and know what you're saying. Always keep in mind that everyone is a potential ally and a potential enemy. Never let your emotions carry the day; you may do more harm than good. The more comfortable and at ease you feel in yourself – the more likely others will feel comfortable around you. Start by doing an excellent job of explaining yourself. If you do this well, it will benefit you in the long run. Never lie to someone; tell them the facts and be honest about your feelings. If you make mistakes, apologize and try to work on fixing them. Don't let others know what makes you feel bad at any time: if they don't care enough to ask, they don't deserve to know.

Others around you must see that there are people who are confident in who they are and how they view the world. Please do your best not to judge others; remember that everyone has a good side and a wrong side, so it's best to keep an open mind when speaking with anyone. Having social skills means gaining the knowledge and confidence to talk with anyone. Being able to communicate with others will not only help you in your career, but it will also help you earn respect and develop lasting friendships. You must convince them there's more to you than meets the eye – they have to see that they can trust you. Speak slowly and carefully – be sure to articulate your words as well as possible. You'll find yourself enjoying time with new people more often, so put these tips into practice as soon as possible.

Here are more tips to help you improve:

1. Listen closely

Pay attention and wait for your turn to speak. It is sometimes frustrating when people don't listen or when they derail a conversation by steering it off-topic. If someone invites you somewhere, respond politely with a yes or no, depending on if your schedule allows it. Don't give an excuse or reason you can't make it because that person will spend the entire night trying to convince you otherwise.

2. Be clear, concise, and to the point.

This doesn't mean you can't be elaborate or involved in the conversation; avoiding going off tangents is essential. When you're talking about something that matters to you, be sure you know where you're heading.

If your message is essential, make others feel it is equally crucial by speaking clearly and confidently. If not, you will appear as if your message is not worth their time and care. Speak with an open mind which includes openness toward other people's ideas and thoughts. When you speak, make your voice heard.

Your voice is an essential tool for communication. Your tone and pitch are what everyone interprets. If your message is unclear, it will sound very dull and unprofessional. So make sure you speak loud enough for everyone to hear you without breaking out into a sweat or whispering, which will only seem like an insult.

3. Pay attention to your body language as well.

When someone speaks to you, they're not looking at you; they're watching you. You may be able to talk, but can you walk the walk? If you don't believe what you are saying, how can others?

Depending on your body language and self-confidence will determine how well you communicate. Stand confidently with your arms at your side. Your body posture should portray confidence. Say what needs to be said without fidgeting or moving around too much.

4. Let others shine as well.

Some people get so caught up in their voices they forget to let others speak. Listening closely is essential, but make sure you are listening and paying attention to the person talking. But it doesn't end there if you are genuinely interested in what another person has to say; your expressions and body language show.
People will value what you say when they see how much value you give to what they say.

The more you practice this technique, the more accessible communication will be. Start by saying "hello" or "how are you?" Remember these tips and notice the difference in how people respond to your words and actions. As you become better at communicating, you will become more confident in yourself and what you have to say. And remember, people will not forget what you said or did, especially when they know it matters most to you. Never forget people will recognize how you interact with them. It is a matter of fact, but it's your choice how you handle those situations.

5. Communicate your thoughts and feelings.

This simple act is what you have to sell and impress others with. However, it may not be that easy. Some people find it difficult to say what's on their minds without putting on a different show.

If you don't feel comfortable sharing your genuine thoughts and emotions, it will be hard for them to believe in you or follow your advice when a problem arises. They may think you are lying or exaggerating a cheap way out of the challenge, but facts are facts; they should know how to react accordingly. Don't compare yourself to others because you will permanently lose in the end; share how good you are now by showing confidence within yourself using this technique.

6. Use the power of visual cues.

Please think of the pictures in your mind and use them to guide your words. For example, if you think of a picture of a mountain, picture yourself as a mountain surrounded by other mountains or wait for the right moment to mention them before you speak about them so that others will feel included and encouraged.

While putting this technique into practice may not be easy, it is something you can do with ease anytime you want to show confidence in yourself and others around you. Be sure not to overlook what others say because they may have valuable advice or suggestions to help build your confidence. It will also help you connect with them and build strong friendships.

A good conversation starter can be the difference between making an impression or just going through the motions. On the other hand, if you don't know how to start a conversation, you probably won't be able to carry one on. Whether during work or in your free time, make sure you are prepared for those conversations by practicing these essential skills and tips for speaking. It is not always easy to know whether to speak or listen because being a good speaker is hard to learn and takes practice. Speaking confidently and skillfully will allow others to see your abilities and trust you with their feelings.

7. Rehearse in advance.

Practice these techniques the day before a big meeting, and memorize everything you want to say. If you do it in advance, you will have time to rehearse when it's time to speak.

When practicing, it is best to visualize yourself standing confidently and confidently speaking your thoughts. Bitterness can creep in if someone talks negatively about what they think of you, even though that person should not have said anything because they do not know you yet.

8. Organize ideas for your speech.

Avoid looking at the floor; look straight ahead or at the person being addressed. Make sure you need to say what you have to say when it is time to speak. If not, let someone else have the floor and step back. This will ensure that those not speaking listen closely to your words by giving them their full attention.

9. Plan to speak last.

It is best to say what you have to say after everyone has had their turn. If you try to put in your two cents before everyone has spoken, your ideas may be misinterpreted as trying to take over the conversation. Instead, stand back and let others say their minds first; listen closely and keep an open mind as they talk. This will allow you to judge what they are talking about and how they feel by the tone of their voice or facial expression. Once you are sure it is your turn to speak, stand confidently in front of the group and deliver your message with clarity and conviction.

Communication should not be an obstacle to building rapport and strengthening relationships. So, the next time you are faced with a situation that requires you to speak with others, remember these tips and use them to your advantage. It is essential to not only listen to others but also hear what they say, so make sure you focus on them and try not to get distracted by your surroundings. Never forget that communication is a two-way street. If you do not listen carefully and attentively, you will never be able to understand what others are telling you.

Chapter 2: Expressing Anger and Managing Conflicts

We all know how difficult it is to talk to someone who consistently makes you angry. Whether they're arrogant or just rude, they can make anyone feel frustrated and lash out at them in return. But instead of conceding to their bad behavior and isolating yourself, you should learn how to communicate with people better — especially when there's a conflict brewing between the two of you.

Communication is key to resolving any conflict. If you can find a way to resolve the issue with someone without breaking down, blaming each other, or losing your temper in the process, you'll make everyone's life easier. When it comes down to it, you'll need to talk through your problems and try to sort everything out with some compromise.

The truth is that talking to someone who makes you angry or frustrated isn't easy. It's hard to remain calm and collected, and your emotions tend to get the best. The hardest part is being able to disagree with them honestly and respectfully. You can't shout or become hostile towards someone if they're going to listen to what you have to say — especially if what you have to say is something they don't want to hear.

Some people may be more challenging to talk to than others (i.e., those who are consistently negative or rude), but there are ways to talk to anyone, regardless of their personality. It might take some time, but you can communicate with any person if you know how.

The essential part of communication has clear, defined boundaries. Have a firm personal limit before talking to someone who makes you angry. Think back to the last time you argued with someone; did they ever try to push your buttons? Were they trying to get you to lose your temper? Or did they wait until you're on the edge of losing it before saying anything?

This is important because refusing to listen or reacting violently when someone pushes your buttons is dangerous and unnecessary. When you know how the other person is trying to manipulate you, you can then choose whether or not you want to listen or fight back.

And even if the other person isn't trying to manipulate you, it's still a good idea to have firm boundaries. If someone keeps pushing your buttons, they're likely trying to make you angry — but if what they're saying isn't affecting how you feel about them, why should you respond with anger?

Once your boundaries are clear and defined, it's much easier for you to talk clearly and respectfully to whoever is making your blood pressure rise. You'll also understand what they're trying to say when they're being rude or pathetic.

Always stand up for yourself (don't let people walk all over you). Lots of people love being rude without even realizing it. Whether it's because they think being condescending or snarky makes them look witty or attractive or because they're too wrapped up in their own lives to care about yours, you shouldn't let other people treat you like crap.

Do you know what's essential? Being a good person and doing right by other people. How you interact with them and how they treat you are equally important; if someone makes your life difficult out of meanness or ignorance, then they don't deserve your forgiveness — especially if the problem could have been easily fixed in the first place.

Don't let people walk all over you. If someone's being disrespectful or hurtful towards you, stand up for yourself as soon as possible. You won't just be making yourself feel better about the situation positively (you'll also be taking away their control over how your day goes). Still, you'll set an excellent example for everyone else to follow and teach them the importance of treating everyone equally.

Keep an open mind. It's easy to get angry when listening to someone who won't stop talking about something that doesn't matter to them or someone who only has bad things to say about everything. It's even easier to be rude or condescending toward them.

But being open-minded and friendly with everyone, no matter how positive their attitudes are, is difficult. It can sometimes get boring to talk to people who only have good things to say. You can't maintain an open-minded attitude towards everyone and everything in life, but you can keep it regarding non-negative people. All they want to do is enjoy their lives and be happy without putting up with terrible attitudes from others (i.e., you). So keep an open mind for a change, regardless of how boring or negative the other person is at times. You never know when something exciting or positive might come out of that conversation after all. If it's hard for you to talk to someone who makes you angry/frustrated, don't feel bad about it.

The more you try to control your anger and frustration, the worse you'll feel — and that's just not healthy. If something is making your blood pressure rise, it's worth trying to figure out what the problem is — and if other people are being rude or hurtful towards you, then, of course, it's worth standing up for yourself in a way that doesn't involve fighting back.

But everyone has had times when they've been frustrated or angry with someone but didn't say anything. Maybe they were scared of what would happen if they did say something (i.e., the other person would react violently), or perhaps they were so angry that they couldn't trust themselves to talk correctly.

It happens to everyone; even the best people in the world have trouble expressing themselves sometimes. If you feel like you can't talk to someone because it's too hard, that's perfectly fine — just focus on becoming a better person in the future and avoid unnecessary arguments with anyone.

Don't let anger consume you. Whether you're trying to communicate with someone who won't listen or if your problems are getting out of hand, remember that losing control isn't worth it — especially when it comes to other people.

Here are some tips on how to communicate better if you are feeling hostile:

1. THINK BEFORE YOU SPEAK

Most of the time, you'll want to speak your mind immediately. But if you have a heated argument with someone (whether it's a coworker, parent, or significant other), you need to make sure that what you're about to say is worth saying. If not, then don't say anything at all.

It's always better to stay silent than speak when you're angry — because the more time passes, the more rational and calm you feel. Don't speak up until you have the facts and can honestly express yourself. You don't have to go off on someone to make a point — you can calmly explain your opinion and tell them why you feel the way you think.

To get yourself to stop and listen to someone, try this trick: Count down from 10 in your head before speaking. By the time you hit zero, you'll be able to express yourself without completely confusing or angering the person on the other end.

2. GET SOME FRESH AIR

If talking about whatever it is that's bothering you makes you feel stressed out or anxious, then take a break from each other instead of continuing the conversation. Do something else for a little while — like take a walk outside or play a game on your phone — and then come back to each other when you're more relaxed.

When it comes down to it, communication is all about two people being able to listen and pay close attention to each other without feeling hostility. Sometimes that's hard to do, so if you're feeling too stressed out, then you'll have a better time if you can just hang out alone for the time being.

3. GET IN THE RIGHT MIND SETTINGS

Sometimes we don't want to hear the truth about a situation because it's too difficult to handle, or we know that what we are about to say will hurt someone's feelings. If you're one of those people, you'll want to ensure that you're in the right frame of mind before speaking to someone.

It's not always easy to do this. You may have to meditate a little bit and clear your head before getting centered. You also need to ensure that you're in a comfortable location, like turning your phone off so that you won't be distracted by any other messages or calls. And if the person making you angry is physically present, try to step away from them and take a break for a little while before attempting to talk things through.

4. LISTEN MORE THAN YOU TALK

You know what to do. You're about to speak your mind, but instead of showing the other person you're upset or angry, try to make a point.

Remember: listening is the best way to get your point across. When you tell someone something, and they interrupt or criticize what you said, it will make them feel more annoyed towards you than ever before. If you can soak in all of what the other person has to say, then there's a greater chance that he'll respect you more for being respectful.

5. BE PATIENT

You shouldn't speak up like a short-tempered older man — that's just going to piss the other person off. If you want to express your feelings, then it's best to try to be as patient as possible. Instead of telling them what you think, try to help the other person understand where they went wrong.

For example: if someone says that they don't like how you did something, you can tell them instead: "I understand. I went faster in turn and lost control of the vehicle."

6. TELL THE TRUTH

Yes, even if it's hard for you to speak about the situation. Even if it hurts to say — especially if it's someone you love or care about deeply — you need to take responsibility for your actions. By not being honest with yourself or the other person, there's no way they will be able to trust or respect you.

There is a time and place for everything, but sometimes life sucks, and things go bad. We tend to say the wrong things and make bad decisions. But it's not about being the wrong person — it's about surviving in a world where people aren't always friendly to each other. And that's okay, as long as you know how to handle yourself and how to act when tempers are running high.

7. ALWAYS HAVE AN EXIT STRATEGY

If things start getting super intense, you need to be able to call a time out — whether that means leaving the room or having the friend with you distract the person on the other end so that you can take some time for yourself.

It's always best if you can handle your feelings without the other person having to know they're affecting you negatively. It's not easy, especially if you want to tell someone something, and no matter how hard you try, it doesn't get said at all.

But the only way to happen is if you have an exit strategy. There's no use in staying in a room if things are terrible. And even if all politics is just a game to you, it doesn't mean that you don't have feelings like everyone else does — and they should be heard as well.

8. BE THE FIRST TO APOLOGIZE

Sometimes life is just messy and complicated when it comes to communication. Sometimes people don't like hearing what you have to say because it hurts them knowing you're upset or angry with them. And sometimes, people take what you say the wrong way without you even knowing.

If this is the case, it's always best if you're the first to apologize — especially if you didn't mean anything wrong to happen in the first place. If there was a misunderstanding, then clear that up as soon as possible by saying sorry.

If there was no misunderstanding, you still need to take responsibility for your actions and say that you never meant for the situation to occur. A quick way to transform hostility into cooperation is to take responsibility for your actions. If you didn't tell, the other person would be mad at you, then say it. If you want to apologize for something, then do it. If you didn't think the situation would go wrong, then say it. Sometimes life is messy and chaotic — and sometimes we say things we don't mean or hear something like that said to us.

If you can apologize for your actions in a way that's calm and honest, then it's likely that the other person will forgive you. And if they don't want to talk to you anymore, then at least you can walk away from the situation knowing that you did everything you could to resolve the conflict peacefully.

The power of empathy and forgiveness
When you know how to express yourself and make the other person feel comfortable, it can be easy to find an understanding and give each other more respect.

We all want people to listen when we talk, but many of us don't know how to do that properly. We're afraid of hurting someone's feelings, and we're too scared to say things that might hurt someone's feelings because we don't want them to think badly about us.

But it doesn't have to be like this. If you can learn how to express yourself well, you can be thoughtful about what you say, even if it makes the other person mad. And this will allow both of you more opportunities in the future.

You never know how much something that seems little could mean something big — especially regarding communication and relationships. People often think it's easier to be empathetic than logical. But using empathy to resolve conflicts gives you the power to turn a negative situation into a positive one. When you can learn how to communicate better with those around you, you'll become more confident and have more power over your life.

Even if you don't always get what you want, at least you can learn when to walk away without having to be held hostage by your own emotions.

The people who stay angry with others are the ones who don't know how to say sorry and accept the feelings of others. And if you're able to use empathy as a gift instead of a weapon, then both sides can try and make peace even if they don't feel like it in the end.

The reality is that most conflicts grow big because people cannot handle them well. Even if you don't like the situation, at least you can learn how to communicate with others in a way that avoids many difficulties.

Suppose you can learn how to have rational conversations that lead to friendly conversations. In that case, you'll be able to resolve conflicts with other people quickly. Communicating better means letting go of your emotions — but you don't have to do it alone. Then you can learn to share without upsetting the other person and without allowing anger to build up inside you until it explodes.

Many people don't like conflict, especially if they think it will leave them angry and stressed out for a long time. But one thing is for sure — if you're going to learn how to get along on any level, then it's necessary for both parties involved.

By learning to communicate better and use empathy instead of anger, you can find a way to turn a negative situation into a positive one. Once you can do that, you can find solutions that you and the other person will be able to live with.

It's not easy — but it is possible to have good relationships with people. All it takes is patience, an open heart, and the ability to communicate your feelings without letting them get in the way. The sooner you learn how to do this, the sooner your life will become more accessible and less stressful — because instead of focusing on the negative things around you, you'll learn how to find solutions for what goes wrong.

Chapter 3: Reading Faces and Predicting Behavior

Your face and your body send out thousands of signals every day. These signals indicate what you are thinking, how you feel, what you want from others, and what you plan to do. These signals are enormously influential in establishing connections, influencing behavior, and achieving goals. You send out these signals without even being aware of it. You constantly read and react to other people's faces and body language, making judgments that affect your feelings, thoughts, and actions.

As soon as you wake up in the morning, you look in the mirror and respond to your facial expressions. Besides impacting how you feel, your facial expressions affect how others think of you. If you are tired, angry, or sad, you will make a negative face that makes you feel worse. Conversely, if you smile at yourself before going off to work or school, it will probably put a smile on your face throughout the day.

Research has proved that how you sit, stand, hold your head, move your hands, and walk can suggest your trustworthiness or competence. Your body also sends out facial signals that others pick up on without your awareness. Open body language—arms uncrossed, palms visible—says "I'm honest and approachable."
Most people, even those with high communication skills, aren't aware of how much they're signaling to each other. You may over- or under-react to someone's facial expressions. Your body language could send mixed messages and make you appear nervous or aggressive even when you're not feeling the old way. You may be unaware of how much you infuriate others by being too direct. How do you know what someone else is thinking?

Your face and body are like a window into the mind, each giving off messages that are hard to decipher on their own. The more you understand how to read people and predict their behavior, the more effective your communication will be.

Reading body language

You should be aware of people's body language so you can better understand their thoughts and feelings. Knowing other people's body language will improve your ability to understand them, predict their actions and behavior, and build strong relationships. You can also use this knowledge to make yourself more appealing as a conversational partner.

People are constantly sending out signals from facial expressions to posture to gestures. The person may scowl, hold his head high, clasp his hands tightly together, look down at the ground or up at the ceiling, and twist his body in. Many alerts are being sent out all the time, which can still be hard for you to read and understand.

You don't have to be a social psychologist or expert in human behavior to read other people's body language correctly. Here are some simple guidelines to help you interpret and respond effectively. People often feel anxious or uncomfortable when they have to interact with others. They usually take several deep, cleansing breaths and tense up their bodies. Watch how people cross their arms, legs, and feet. They may tuck their hands under their armpits or cross their legs in front of them. Be aware of what people do with their hands because they send out necessary signals when they put them in certain positions.

Pacing is a sign of nervousness or anticipation. When you see someone pacing around the room, you can assume that they are apprehensive about something upcoming. If you get up to go to the bathroom during a job interview, notice how the interviewer's body language and behavior change as soon as you leave the room.

Don't overlook the importance of posture and facial expression to indicate what someone is thinking. People tend to follow one another's lead unconsciously, so if your boss sits behind his desk and crosses his legs, you will follow suit and do the same thing. You know that now it is time for business, not casual conversation.

The next time you're in a public place like a restaurant or theater, pay attention to how people react when they walk into a group. They will usually find a place to sit halfway between the most dominating and weakest people. If you are in a meeting, try to observe the seating arrangements. People usually sit next to people they like or are comfortable with.

The next time you're at a party, listen carefully to what people say when they introduce themselves to someone new. Very few people will say anything negative about themselves, even though they may talk negatively about others. Observe how casually people shake hands. The stronger the grip, the more dominant and confident they feel while shaking hands with you—which may indicate how tough they really are.

You can use the same technique for another reason: to see how confident people are about a specific topic or subject. If you know what mood a person is in, you will have an easier time guessing what he might be talking about when introductions are made.

Before you go out with friends the next time, watch how much weight one person distributes evenly across his feet and hands as he walks so that his center of gravity is nice and even. He will walk like he has nothing to prove. If you ever get into an argument with someone, and he tries to pick either one of your hands up at the wrist, it tells you he is feeling vulnerable and insecure about something.

When greeting someone, look at his feet and notice how they're pointed. If they are pointed toward you, it is a sign of openness and confidence; if they are pointed away from you, it is a sign of rejection or defensiveness. Watch how straight a person stands up when talking to someone he's attracted to. He will stand much more straightforwardly than usual because he will try to look as attractive as possible.

When people stand with their arms crossed in front of them, this is a sign that they are blocking themselves off from the world. They feel turned off by what's happening around them and are not interested in getting involved in anything that might happen. People who cross their arms in front of them often do it because they feel vulnerable, insecure, or insecure about something.

A person who leans his face toward you to talk may be trying to get closer to you physically or may just be emphasizing what he is saying by extending himself outward. The opposite is true when a person pulls away from you and crosses his arms tightly with his hands in fists. These are signs that this person was not receptive to your ideas then.

Here are five body language tips:

1.) Keep your feet planted on the floor while talking to someone else unless walking is necessary. The more comfortable and confident you appear, the more others will be drawn to you.
2.) Smile and laugh often, even if you don't feel like it. Even if you are not having a good day, make a conscious effort to force yourself to smile more. A smile is one of the best ways to make others feel good about themselves and for you to come across as a warm, caring person.
3.) Make sure that your eyes are focused on the other person and that your head is at an angle (not straight up or down). These two things will help show your interest in what the other person is saying and help move the conversation along more smoothly.
4.) If you find yourself in situations where someone else's body language sends negative signals, do not mirror them. If you push back by crossing your arms, leaning away from someone, or turning down your neck and facial expression, you're only making yourself look like a less confident person. You will make it harder for the other person to be drawn toward you and feel comfortable.
5.) Pay attention to the way that people talk in a light and friendly tone (never using the word "like" or "as if"). Remember that no one will notice any minor changes you make on your own. The most important thing is to listen intently, not just hear what others are saying.

Body language can be divided into three general categories: behavioral, ritual, and emotional. Here is an example of how each category would be read:

Behavioral—A person in this category would approach you with a friendly smile, open stance, hands on hips, leaning slightly forward, and shaking or tapping their foot in rhythm.

Ritual—This person may stroll to get closer to your conversation with exaggerated hand gestures or fingernail polish. He may rub his chin the entire time you talk and turn his head slowly from side to side like a bird looking for worms.

Emotional—The person in this category may move closer to you, lean their face toward yours, or open their hands and place them on your arm when he talks to you. He may be afraid of something or unsure of what he is saying.

The key to reading body language is to tune into all three categories by looking for signs from each type. Of course, we want to ensure that we're picking up on the non-verbal cues, not what someone said. By understanding these concepts, you'll be a better judge of what's happening around you and better understand how to gauge people's moods and responses.

When someone is speaking, study the way their mouth moves. Does it move too fast or too slow? Does it open wide at certain intervals? What are their hands doing during the conversation? Do the person's arms move in a coordinated manner with their speech, or are they swinging wildly back and forth as they talk?

You should also pay attention to whether their facial expressions match the words they're saying. Does their mouth seem to be grinning, frowning, or smiling? What eyebrow patterns are they using? Are they making sudden changes in their expression?

A person expressing much emotion while someone else is speaking to them will often lean forward or turn away from you and make sudden loud noises. If the person's face turns red or whatever color their face turns, this is a clear sign that they want to be left alone.

This sign can be easily seen by scientists and researchers studying stereotypes. They have noticed a correlation between how long a person has been doing something before performing it perfectly and the time it takes for him to get good at it. If a person has been doing something for ten years and is still not very good at it, it is a sign that they have not been applying to it.
Here are essential things to remember when reading body language:

1. Be skeptical of everything you read. Your first reaction when hearing a piece of body language advice will be to agree with it completely. If you take yourself out of the picture and attempt to apply that same bit of information to another person, however, you'll be able to tell if it is useful.
2. Don't focus on one person and expect them to give off specific body language cues all day. Instead, be sensitive and feel what's going on around you while also working on keeping your body language in check.
3. Do not engage in stereotypes. This is a big no-no in reading body language because stereotypes are dangerous. If someone is telling you something is true based on their color, gender, sexual orientation, or any other type of bias, then you do not want to believe it.

4. Pay attention to non-verbal cues as well as verbal ones. Saying anything can be said in non-verbal language, and if you're able to pick up on these cues, it will make understanding how someone's body language works that much easier for you.
5. Let people speak when they wish and listen more than talk. When someone is speaking to you, do not interrupt unless you have something significant to add. When someone is speaking, move your body and facial muscles to show that you are listening.
6. Always remember that everyone has a story to tell. You may have an opinion about what's happening with another person, but if they don't want to talk to you or make eye contact with you, then do not persist in prying them for information. It will only get in the way of them telling their story on their own time and probably ruin it.
7. Only observe touching if you feel comfortable with it. When you see someone touch another person, this is a clear sign that they are satisfied with them and feel safe around them. This is not something that everyone wants to do, and it's not something that everyone should do, so don't force yourself into physical contact with anyone who you don't feel is willing to give it to you.
8. Do not judge people until you know their backgrounds and why they act the way they do. Remember, everyone has a story to tell, but only they know how it will end up for them in the future.
9. Let go of any baggage you may have. If you have a history with someone, allow him or her the opportunity to show you his or her new side even though they might not seem to be the same person as they once were or even the same person you once knew.

10. If you see something wrong, do not be afraid to speak up. Have an opinion of what's going on around you or with one person and say something rather than making a judgment on your own. Remember, everyone is flawed.

In this day and age, it is essential to understand people's nonverbal behavior. Reading faces and predicting behavior based on nonverbal cues can be difficult, but it is worth it if you want to improve your interpersonal interactions. Otherwise, you might make many mistakes that could have been avoided. The key to the successful reading of body language is to remember what you see and what others see and that different people will react differently to the same situation. Each person has their version of the truth, and you must learn how to adapt yourself to read their body language effectively.

Nonverbal cues are important because they are one of the main ways that people communicate with each other. By reading their nonverbal cues, you'll be able to understand the situation and how to respond to it. You'll also be able to tell how that person is feeling and what they will say next. While it may seem daunting at first, the skill of reading body language is not as difficult as it looks. Once you improve, you'll find that understanding other people's body language feels much more natural. You will be able to see the hidden cues and understand their responses instantly without any difficulty or misunderstanding. You will feel confident in your ability to read body language and know exactly how to act based on your nonverbal cues.

Chapter 4: Giving and Receiving Feedback

Feedback is a vital component of effective communication. It is central to understanding what is happening in the conversation and ensuring that both parties are represented. When feedback becomes difficult, it comes down to a lack of confidence and practice. Feedback is a critical component of any negotiation or relationship; your ability to give and receive feedback makes the difference in negotiating for better deals, getting a job done, or making a sale. It is the skill that helps you to improve your skills and make you a better salesperson.

Feedback is vital to effectively communicate with others because it allows you to respond appropriately. Feedback is the difference between "I think you are wrong" and "You are wrong." Using the feedback that someone has given you allows you to learn how others perceive situations differently than yourself. Feedback also enables you to remember what someone has said rather than assume they are telling the truth as they see it, which can be detrimental to negotiations.

Feedback is a skill that cannot be perfected overnight, but with practice, it will become an integral part of your communication style.

Step 1: Critique the performance of others.

Learn from your feedback and remember when making your subsequent evaluation. Having critiques done on yourself may be difficult, but when you start critiquing others, avoid putting your personal feelings into it and focus on the facts of their performance when making your evaluations. Evaluate them by their performance, not their personalities.

Step 2: Learn to listen to others effectively.

Learn how to listen to get more information and clear communication necessary to be successful in any interaction. Listening is an essential skill to learn when working with others, as it allows you to understand what the other person is saying. When listening, you should: 1) Listen to interruptions, 2) not make judgments based on your perspective, and 3) Take time to understand what is being said. For example, if someone says, "The meeting was terrible. The room was too cold." You may respond emotionally to the comment and ask, "which room?" or "What was wrong with the meeting?" The person may say that the client wanted a warmer environment, and you did not deliver it. This statement may be a request for feedback from you that you can use to help improve your next interaction.

Step 3: Practice active listening skills.

Active listening is another essential skill that helps you get information about what is happening in the interaction. Active listening allows you to understand whether what someone is saying is true. For example, when someone is talking, you should: 1) Be fully engaged in the conversation, 2) Make eye contact with the speaker, 3) Understand their feelings and opinions by reflecting them to them, and 4) Take notes on what is being said. To effectively communicate your ideas, it is important to listen well.

Step 4: Be fully engaged in the conversation.

Being fully engaged allows the other person to feel that they are being heard and that they are being given your complete attention. It can also make people think that you do not want to be there and will not be a productive interaction. Staring at your phone or checking a watch without the effort to be involved in the discussion can be construed as disinterest and disconnection.

Step 5: Understand their feelings and opinions by reflecting on them.

When you are listening empathetically, it allows the other person to feel that they have been heard. By putting their feelings into words, the person cannot help but have those words reflected on them. You should mirror or empathize with what the speaker is saying by using "I see" or "I understand." This will give the speaker a sense of being understood and erase any chances they may have misunderstood or misinterpreted.

Step 6: Take notes on what is being said.

Taking notes during an interaction to summarize what is being said will help you to remember the discussion and keep you focused on what is being discussed. Taking notes will help you focus more on the conversation and improve your active listening skills. It will also allow you to review what was agreed upon, which may be helpful for follow-up or future communications with the person.

When to use feedback

"When to tell someone that they are wrong? It is important to always recognize that people make mistakes. You should always provide feedback when they do something wrong. The worst thing you can do is not identify when someone makes a mistake or have access to feedback when trying to improve. The right time frame varies depending on the situation, but it should be within your first few interactions with someone."

Receiving feedback is essential in making you a better communicator. Receiving feedback allows you to understand how others see situations differently and help you define better what works and what does not work for them. Receiving feedback can also help you improve your skills and make you a better communicator.

Reflect on feedback when someone gives you feedback and ask them for clarification. This will allow you to understand what they mean. Taking time to reflect on the feedback will help you to improve your communication skills.

Here are some things that you should do to receive feedback:

1.) Have a purpose for the meeting before and during. Know why you will be talking with this person. For example, if you are meeting with a customer service representative and are dissatisfied with their performance, understanding why it is essential that this person is there will improve your interaction.
2.) When making requests of others, make sure that your request is for a specific action to get an accurate response from them. It may be helpful to define the incident or situation to clarify what you want the other person to do and prevent misinterpretation of your request. For example, "I would like to have my order shipped by noon. It is evening, and I have not received a shipment confirmation or tracking number."
3.) Listen to what the other person has to say. Their suggestions and comments may provide you with information you did not know about the situation.

4.) Summarize what you heard from the other person to clarify the message that you heard from them. After listening, reflect on their feedback by summarizing what you hear them saying so that they can confirm or deny your summary. This will allow for a clear understanding of their thoughts and opinions.

5.) Repeat any critical information so they can verify whether or not you understood what they were trying to say. Repeating back to them will prevent you from leaving out any important messages.

6.) Verify that they agree that the issue has been resolved by asking them, "Did I do a good job with this feedback?" or "Is this something that we can agree on as being resolved?" This will allow the other person to verify whether or not you truly understood and "fixed" their problem.

7.) Thank the other person for their time and feedback to show your gratitude for their interaction. Showing gratitude will help you maintain a positive relationship with this person, and they may be more likely to work with you again.

How and where to provide feedback

"Knowing how to give feedback is important when working with other people. Knowing how you should give feedback will help you ensure that you are getting your point across and that the other person knows that you are trying to improve the business or whatever situation you may be in. Feedback might not always be positive, but it is essential to growing as a professional and ensuring that your work is fulfilling its purpose."

We give and receive feedback in many places in our everyday lives. Giving feedback can happen anywhere from a classroom setting to online social media interactions. We often communicate through written and verbal means in our day-to-day lives. For example, oral and written communication can give feedback at work.

Setting up an informal or formal meeting will lead to how you deliver your feedback. A formal meeting may require more questions than employees' relaxed, friendly atmosphere. If you are taking notes for a forum in which the input will be given, make sure you consider the other person's situation and the tone of the discussion.

When you receive feedback, you may be excited about your progress and feel that you have done a great job, but it is essential to remember that receiving feedback is not always the goal. You can still be thankful for the input and not let it become a distraction from what is happening in your life.

Here are some tips on how to provide feedback:

1.) Look for the best way to provide feedback so it will be received correctly by the other person. Here are some ways that you can give feedback:
a.) Directly put your thoughts into the world so they will be heard and understood by the other person.
b.). Illustrate your thoughts and concerns through examples from a situation you are working on.

c.) Sharing written notes of things you have observed or done will help express your understanding of the situation. You can read these tweets or emails to the other person and let them know through these notes of your observations about their work or feedback about work that you feel is important.

2.) Read each person's reaction - to see whether or not they understood what was said. If not, re-word it in a way that is clear and easy to understand for the other person.

3.) Question if the other person feels the same way. This is essential to ensuring that you are on the same page and truly understand what they are trying to say and want.

4.) Thank them for their time and their opinion. This will show your gratitude for what they have said and done.

5.) Make sure that you think about what was said to you and reflect on it. Use this as a way to improve yourself as a communicator in the future by seeing your own mistakes and noticing how other people communicate with you.

6.) Remember that feedback is not just something that happens at work, but you give and receive feedback in your everyday life. Critique your communication with others to become a better listener and communicator.

7.) How do you give feedback? What tips would you like to share with other people?"

Feedback is often seen as a necessary evil in most situations, although it can be a valuable tool. There are many ways that feedback can be effective, both positive and negative. Below we will discuss how to use feedback effectively in various situations.

Positive Feedback

Positive feedback is a great way to compliment someone for doing their job well and providing good customer service. Positive feedback also encourages the other person to do their best work because of your positive attitude toward them. Having this type of relationship with your coworkers can help you become a stronger team player and leader within an organization. Use this situation to share a positive note with your coworkers by simultaneously using both positive and negative feedback. It is important to note that both types of feedback should be delivered with a friendly attitude and an understanding of the situation.

When giving positive feedback, it is a good idea to provide examples of what you have seen that person do well for others in your organization and customers. This will show your employees and team members that you are paying attention to their work and still showing them that you appreciate their efforts daily.

Giving negative feedback will help to show that you are not afraid to speak up and honestly express your concerns about the product, the process, or the employee. Negative feedback should be delivered in a friendly manner, as well as a professional manner. Negative feedback is often used to ensure that employees perform their jobs correctly and do what they are told to do. Therefore, negative feedback should always be given with an understanding of how some products or services can end up being a problem for customers in the long run.

Accordingly, negative feedback can be crucial for an organization to understand why certain products are not working out for their customers. Also, it becomes easier to fix the problem and improve on them so that they will work correctly in the future. Negative feedback can be given in many forms: verbal feedback, written notes, and feedback through social media. This can help to show that you are taking the time to give your employees feedback during a meeting, but also through other methods of communication.

Please note that negative feedback can sometimes be difficult for employees. Try not to give negative feedback through email or phone because these mediums can make it seem like you are just not interested in them or their work. Additionally, most employees will become defensive when criticized because of how highly they usually view themselves compared to their coworkers. It can be a good idea to avoid giving negative feedback in person.

One of the best ways to understand how you should give negative feedback is to ask your friends or coworkers what they have seen from you or others in your company. Ask them to share with you both positive and negative aspects of their jobs so that you can see what types of things you do that are acceptable and not acceptable for the organization. This can help you to be more effective when giving critical feedback because it will not appear like you are only speaking negatively about someone's performance when in reality, there are many different ways that people can improve their work product.

When discussing negative feedback with your employees, try not to use too much emotion in your verbal communication. This can help your employees not feel so defensive about what you are saying and will help you be a better listener. Open up the conversation between you and your employee about the negative feedback by asking them how they feel about their work, products, or services they deliver to customers. This way, you can open up a dialogue with them before giving your feedback so that they do not feel like they have been blindsided by it. This will also allow them to understand you better as a leader and help the employee understand where their performance is going wrong in certain situations.

Chapter 5: Building Rapport, Networking, and Creating a Unique Personality

Rapport is a vital communication skill. It requires giving the other person your full attention and being interested. Additionally, it's about matching their body language, attitude, and tone of voice. Rapport puts the other person at ease, helping them to talk freely. You get to know them better, they like you more, and they're more likely to share their true thoughts and feelings. People with rapport often feel comfortable giving each other honest feedback and are more effective leaders. The proper rapport can also help you get new clients, friends, or a job interview; create a relaxed working environment, and even make you appear more attractive.

Learning how to build rapport is a skill that can be learned. You can listen actively, ask questions and take an interest in the other person by making statements based on what they tell you. Rapport takes practice, but it's worth it.

Rapport is built on the level of trust between two people. The more rapport you have, the deeper the trust. Understand that trust can be misplaced and fade rapidly when someone realizes they've been misled. Rapport is built by giving straightforward answers, being honest, and not promising anything you can't deliver. As a result, people will feel safe with you, contributing to their comfort level with your presence and ability to share feedback freely.

To make the most of rapport, you should know your audience and which types of people you're likely to encounter. Consider using the information you've gained to make an excellent first impression. Adapt your body language and tone of voice to the other person's demeanor. Use their words when asking questions and mirror their gestures, facial expressions, and gestures to create a connection with them.

Use the conversation as an opportunity to assess the other person. If they seem distracted or are avoiding eye contact, it might be because they don't like what they hear from you, or they see little or no value in what you have to offer them. In this case, you should listen to what they say and adjust your behavior accordingly. Don't be afraid to respond briefly and then move on unless they ask a question that requires you to elaborate.

The best way to know how someone will react is to watch them without coming across as too interested—don't be pushy or try too hard. The best way to find out about people is by asking questions and listening closely for the answers. This will help you find essential information about them, but only after the person has spoken. When you need more information, ask again later when the person is more relaxed or open. Your questions don't have to be complicated. A simple "How are you?" will have the other person speaking freely to you. You can ask follow-up questions such as, "What do you like best about your job?" Then listen attentively to their responses.

The best way to build rapport is by practicing with your family, friends, or anyone you care about. The next time someone brings a new person into the group—someone who seems shy or awkward—ask them about themselves and get them involved in the conversation immediately. The more experience you get, the easier it will be to build rapport with people at work or in your personal life.

Rapport is a vital communication skill that can be used not just to make others feel more comfortable but yourself. As you get to know the other person better and can build a strong relationship with them, they'll open up and be more forthcoming with their feelings and thoughts. This will help you see things from their perspective, judge their feelings or ideas, and make better decisions. With your newfound insight, you will then be able to connect with your customers or clients on a much deeper level than before.

Rapport is simple but complex. Building it takes practice and patience. It would be best if you worked at it and practiced often. The more you use it, the easier it will become. Understanding what's going on in a person's mind is difficult because many people are closed-minded and don't freely share their feelings. This can be because they feel threatened by someone who wants something from them or wants to keep their personal life private.

The best way to build rapport with people is by listening actively, paying attention, keeping your gestures and tone of voice appropriate for each individual, and then mirroring those gestures and body language when talking with them.

Benefits of building rapport.
- It increases your chances of getting what you want.

- It helps you get along better and be more productive at work.
- It improves your stress level by making you feel good.
- It makes new relationships easier to manage and grow.
- It can help you achieve more in less time because people will trust you more and be willing to listen when you speak.

Therefore, building rapport is essential to be successful in any business or personal relationship.

The first stage in building a rapport is adjusting our body language, facial expressions, and posture to the other person's demeanor. We need to make sure that we control our voices so that we do not lose control of our emotions, as this is a potent tool to have in our arsenal.

The second part of building a rapport with people is making them feel comfortable enough to open up and tell us how they think, their likes and dislikes, their hopes and dreams, and even the things they don't like so that we can get to the core of who they are. Since ancient times, people have used body language to build rapport with others. When you make that rapport, you're more likely to get what you want from them, and your communication becomes more effective. Therefore, adjusting your voice, body language, and posture to the other person makes it easier for them to open up and express themselves. Your body language is a potent tool in building that rapport.

The next part is about listening actively. You should begin by standing up and keeping your hands loose at your sides. You need to face the conversation and have good eye contact with the other person, not stare at them but look into their eyes and then turn your head away to increase the amount of time you look into them.

Networking

Networking is the process of introducing yourself to or building connections with people to explore opportunities for advancing your knowledge, professional skills, and career.

The primary benefit of networking is the opportunity to expand your network of contacts. In this instance, you obtain information, advice, or referrals that would otherwise likely be outside your contact's circle. Expanding your network also increases the likelihood of finding mentors and job opportunities. By boosting your social circle, you also expand your reach in many aspects of life and personal relationships.

There are many methods for networking. One of the most common is a combination of in-person, telephone, and online networking. Online and telephone networking are often used in conjunction with each other, while in-person meetings are used with phone and online meetings if necessary. People can choose to use any or all three methods to best suit their needs and schedule, but there is not one method that is more effective or productive than another.

Some advantages of expanding your network include the following:

- Allowing you to work on your own time.
- Promoting face time instead of phone time.

- Expanding your social circle.
- Making new professional connections (or maintaining old ones).
- Increasing your visibility and opportunities.
- Meeting new people involved in the same business or field as you.
- Gathering information and advice.
- Being able to make connections that have influenced those who matter most to your professional goals (people who have influence can be people who can help you get a job, advance in your career, or be more successful).

As you expand your network of contacts, you can discover a wealth of information and relationships that could benefit you in every area of life. Expanding your social circle, for instance, makes it easier to make new professional connections or maintain the ones you already have if necessary.

Networking is done by many people of all ages, including entrepreneurs, professionals, job seekers, and students. Whether you are looking to advance in your career or build a professional network for other reasons, networking is a great way to expand your circles and make new connections.

When networking, it is essential to focus on building relationships instead of only business transactions. People who focus just on business transactions tend to come across as insincere and uninterested in the relationship itself, which can end up closing doors instead of opening them.

This doesn't mean that you should always be the one giving the advice instead of taking advice from others; it means you should give without expecting anything in return. It would be best to focus on the relationship instead of solely on yourself. Your actions, such as providing advice to others, helping out with projects, and volunteering your skills, can help you gain their trust. It is also essential for you to maintain consistent contact with others in the networking community.

It would be best if you didn't overdo your networking to maintain a good image and professional contacts. To establish credibility and build a solid professional network, you must do many things that cannot be done over the phone or through email.

It is possible to network successfully in various ways:

- Make sure you maintain contact with those in your network by keeping in touch regularly through phone calls or e-mails.
- Put together a list of your contacts and the contacts' contact information.
- Make sure that you keep your list and contact information up-to-date so that it is easy for people to get in touch with you.
- Be sure to inform those around you about your network by introducing them to those you might have met who could help them.
- Use social media websites such as Facebook or Linkedin to connect with others.
- Put out a general call for new contacts through one or more professional networking sites, such as LinkedIn.

- Use networking groups to introduce yourself and make contacts in the business, social, or professional community.

Networking is a great way to get the support you need to advance your career. It can be one of the most rewarding things you do in your personal and professional life. As you begin networking, it is essential to remember that networking is all about building relationships with others. When making these relationships, you must take care of yourself and not burn bridges by being too pushy or obnoxious toward others.

Personalities and Forecasting Behavior
Communication is one of the most critical aspects of workplace success. Effective communication is also a significant factor in workplace relationships. Communication can often help build better relationships in the workplace, but it can also destroy those relationships daily. As human beings, we are not entirely alike, and we all have unique personalities. Many factors, such as family upbringing and childhood experiences, have shaped our personalities since birth. Personalities are a big part of how people view themselves and perceive others. Your personality also affects your communication style, which can significantly impact how others perceive you at and outside work.

The personalities of the people you work with can play a significant role in how you experience your relationships within the workplace. Over the years, four personality traits have been identified: conscientiousness, openness to experience, extraversion, and agreeableness. Openness to experience is a factor that is associated with curiosity, artistry, and tolerance. This trait also relates to abstract thinking, intellect, and knowing what makes you happy. Extraversion is marked by social skills and being outgoing in public situations or with others.

Extraverts are often self-confident and enthusiastic about their personalities and those around them. Other traits related to extraversion include talkative, assertive, and energetic behavior. Then there is agreeableness which is marked by a sense of being cooperative, kind, and helpful toward others. Agreeable people will tend to be polite and cooperative towards others, while they may not be as assertive or confident as people who are extroverts.

These personality traits can profoundly affect your workplace relationships, especially if they do not fit with the personalities of your co-workers. Certain personality traits, such as being highly conscientious, open to new experiences, and having weak social skills, will negatively impact your work performance. All of these traits can put you at risk for stress in the workplace.

Highly conscientious and conscientious people are generally of good character and do not need much hand-holding or assistance when learning new things. They will often be quick learners and prefer to work alone instead of working with others in the workplace. They also have a strong work ethic, which will often translate into being highly respectful towards the importance of the job that they are doing in the workplace. Therefore, creating a unique personality in the workplace is one of the most important factors to consider.

Being highly conscientious does not mean being a workaholic but merely being responsible and accountable for the way you manage your time. People who choose to be highly moral can quickly become stressed at work if no strategic plan is implemented for them. These individuals are hardworking and have exceptional skills in working towards personal goals.

Highly conscientious people can be easily bored if they do not have a plan of action laid out in front of them to work on. One of the best ways to keep motivated is by setting goals for yourself which will assist you in meeting those goals. Always include your co-workers in your goals since their ideas and assistance can help motivate you to complete those tasks with less effort or stress.

If you are working with a conscientious person in your workplace, try to delegate assignments and tasks that will help promote their growth at the job they have been assigned. If workers have questions about their duties or the task they are working on, they need to keep asking questions until all of the details have been worked out.

When dealing with highly conscientious people, you should keep meetings short. They may seem hesitant when it comes to meetings because they prefer to work independently from others instead of in groups or teams. This can be problematic since they will not be able to share their ideas and opinions with others, leading to an ineffective work relationship between you.

Chapter 6: The Foundations of Communication, the Forms It Takes, and the Elements That Comprise It

Communication is difficult. There are many ways to communicate, but we all know it's not as simple as learning a particular language and practicing. Communication is complex and vast. It requires much work, effort, and planning to get good at it.

What are the foundations of communication?

Foundations of communication are the techniques, skills, and behaviors used to convey one's thoughts, ideas, or emotions to another person. They are the things we learn and practice on a day-to-day basis to be good at communicating effectively. The foundation of communication is, first, how to listen; second, how to read someone's facial expressions; and third, how to speak or write about what's on your mind.

Listening

The first step in communication is listening. You can't communicate if you don't have a place you're talking from. One of the essential skills that are required for us to communicate effectively is the ability to listen. Listening isn't easy, but it's not impossible, either. It would be best to be attentive and alert to what people around you say or do. Being cautious and conservative will help you listen, but being present is key in communication. You must also be able to make yourself available, which means you have to be available when they need you. Being known is an essential skill in communicating effectively at any time.

You need to understand and put yourself in the other person's shoes before you can truly understand what they're trying to tell you. Additionally, you have to be able to take what the other person is saying and put it into your own words. Lastly, you have to remember your manners while listening. This includes staying quiet while they're talking, nodding when they're finished speaking, being respectful, etc.

Communicating effectively sometimes also means controlling how much we talk as well. It shouldn't be all about us, but rather a mutual exchange of ideas and understanding between two people. We should listen twice as much as we speak for our communication with each other to satisfy both parties involved.

Reading facial expressions

The second step in communication informs readers about what an individual thinks or feels by reading their facial expressions. The face is a tool that we all use to communicate with others. It's a potent tool, but it's also very misunderstood. Facial expressions are made up of muscles that surround the mouth, eyes, and nose. These muscles sometimes play tricks on us and misrepresent the feelings and thoughts that they're associated with. For example, when talking to someone, and their face becomes flushed red, many assume that the other person is angry or upset with them. However, there are many reasons for a flushed face, including temperature control (it could be hot in an office or other area), alcohol (if the person is drunk), embarrassment (if the person is ashamed about something), etc. If we wait to read the face and let our intuition kick in, we risk missing out on important things that someone is trying to tell us.

Reading a person's facial expressions is an essential skill to have to communicate effectively with different people. For us to be able to do this successfully, we need to be able to look at an individual's face and determine what it means. You have to put yourself in their shoes and think about it from their perspective before understanding what they're trying to tell you. Again, this requires being attentive and alert at all times, as well as keeping our minds open and understanding the possible emotions of another person.

Speaking or writing about what's on your mind

The third step of communication is all about communicating with others. The people around us can't read facial expressions but can read our minds. If we could share our thoughts and ideas through words, it would be up to other people to decide how we express ourselves. Again, this requires being always attentive and alert, but it also requires that we be able to express ourselves. Being able to express yourself is an important skill for communicating effectively. You must be able to speak and write clearly and coherently if you want others around you to understand what you're trying to say. To do this, we need patience with ourselves and to accept our mistakes from time to time. We should always strive to improve our writing and speaking skills, but if we try too hard or get frustrated, it can be the opposite of the result we're looking for.

Communicating effectively with others is essential to making our world a better place. Communication is vital in our everyday lives, but it's not easy. It requires a lot of work and effort to make it work, but being good at communicating can be very rewarding.

The forms that Communication takes

Communication can be formal or informal. A proper conversation requires a structure when two or more people are talking together. An informal conversation is used between two parties when they know each other well enough to understand how they will communicate.

- Formality: Formality is the level of formality of a communication situation. It influences how the result of communication will be perceived by those in attendance and those watching it on television.
- Informality: Informality is the level of informality or non-formalness in which communication occurs. This can be influenced by the situation, the audience, the formality of the situation, and the parties in communication.
- Formal vs. Informal: Formal is how language is structured; it is the standard language used in any communication situation involving two or more people. The informal nature of communication can be a significant factor influencing the outcome of communication. Informal conversation occurs between people who know each other very well and are comfortable sharing their thoughts, ideas, and feelings.

The elements that comprise communication
The following are communication elements and how they can be applied in various situations.
Five Elements of Communication:

1) Verbal and non-verbal communication: Verbal/Non-verbal communication occurs whenever an individual speaks and listens to another person verbally (words). Non-verbal communication occurs whenever an individual is not speaking or listening but can still communicate through touch, gesture, and body language. This means that non-verbal communication involves more than just the voice. It also requires attitude, posture, and movement.
2) Information exchange: The information exchange refers to the type of information being communicated, who it is from, and what it involves. The information exchanged or transmitted can be verbal (words), written (letters, e-mails, texts, etc.), or non-verbal. The information exchange can also be formal, informal, or formal and informal, depending on the situation. The type of information that is received from others is referred to as feedback.
3) Message: A message is any form of communication that you have given to someone else, either verbally (in person), written (via paper, email, or text), or non-verbally (body language). The sender sends out the message, and then it's received by the receiver. The receiver does not see what message was sent until they open it up and read it themselves. They will then interpret and understand the message, allowing them to respond. The response that they give can be verbal or non-verbal. It depends on how they interpret and understand what they read or hear. The answer can be agreement, support, dissent, or even confusion.

4) Feedback: Feedback is the response to the sender or individual who initially initiated the message. This is what determines how effective of a communicator you are. You should always listen to this feedback and take it at face value because it's an essential part of the communication process. Feedback should always be used to improve your communication skills.
5) Formal vs. Informal: The formal vs. informal communication element refers to the formality level at which a message is sent and received. The story of formality can be impacted by the situation, audience, and type of information being exchanged between individuals. Formal communication occurs when you communicate with someone you do not know well or have never met before. It also appears when you are communicating with someone who has power over you (e.g., manager, teacher, doctor, etc.) Informal communication takes place between people who know each other very well and can talk freely about anything they want to talk about at that moment. The informal nature of communication can be a significant factor influencing the outcome of communication.

Communication is essential in our everyday lives. It's up to us to take the time and effort to make sure that we are good at communicating with one another. It takes patience, tact, and a lot of practice, but being a good communicator will benefit you greatly in the future.

Be discreet and polite when communicating with others. The worst thing you can do is insult someone or make them feel bad while talking. Always be patient and listen carefully because communication is different for everyone, so it's essential not to take things personally when communicating with other people. Practice making small talk whenever you can. Whenever you go to a social or business event, get the opportunity to meet new people.

Chapter 7: The BIGGEST Mistakes People Make When Communicating

When communicating with people, we often do things that sabotage our communication efforts. When you do the following items, people get defensive and start to shut down and tune you out, which completely defeats the purpose of trying to communicate. But when you're in control of your own emotions and clearly understand other people's needs, you can become better at talking to anyone with anything.

You make errors in verbal communication. The common verbal communication errors that most of us make are as follows:

Mistake #1. You don't listen to what they're saying - when talking with someone, and you tend to take your thoughts and feelings hostage in the conversation instead of letting them speak. As a result, your mind starts wandering off into plans for the future or other ideas.

Mistake #2. You don't pick up their body language. They think you're not listening to them when you don't pick up on their body language. It's essential to read people's verbal and non-verbal communication.

Mistake #3. You don't clarify your thoughts. When speaking with someone, it's important to make sure that you know exactly what your intentions are - and you have to be very clear about your thoughts. Otherwise, the person won't know where their thoughts stand, which will cause them to start thinking about other things.

Mistake #4. You're not empathetic toward them. When you're not compassionate toward them, they feel they can't be open with you and share their honest thoughts and feelings. As a result, they shut down and tend to build up walls between themselves and others where they close off their true intentions.

Mistake #5. You don't have a solid understanding of their needs. When you don't have a strong knowledge of the person's needs, you don't know what to say or how to act when talking with them. You may end up saying something that completely offends them without realizing it.

When communicating with people, we often do things that sabotage our communication efforts. But when you're in control of your own emotions and clearly understand other people's needs, you can become better at talking to anyone with anything.

Mistake #6. You don't have a solid understanding of your own needs. When you don't understand your needs, you can develop feelings that cause a lot of tension in your body. As a result, when you're talking with someone, and things start getting emotional, you can lose control over your emotions and say something that might offend them or hurt their feelings.

Mistake #7. You're not aware of the other person's emotions. When you're not aware of the other person's emotions, it makes it difficult for them to explain what they feel to you because they can never develop the same awareness about their feelings in others around them. In a case like this, people tend to become defensive about their feelings because they don't fully understand them.

Mistake #8. You don't clearly understand what you want to achieve with them. When it comes to talking with someone, there are two primary goals we have to keep in mind:

    a. Get them to open up and be aware of their feelings and thoughts.
    b. To get them to be able to see us for who we are.
    c. To do this, we have to have a solid understanding of our goals with others and how to talk in a way that persuades them toward those goals.

We need to make sure that we're making progress in our communication. We need to be coming from a place of wanting the other person's help and the best outcome possible, not just asking for something.

Mistake #9. This is one of the biggest mistakes we make when communicating with others. You don't clearly understand the outcome you're trying to achieve. The product should be beneficial for both parties. Otherwise, there's no real point in talking about it with them in the first place.

Mistake #10. You don't clearly understand how to communicate with people who are different from you. When you communicate with people who are different from yourself, you need to be aware that these people have another way of thinking and feeling about things than you do - and they may need more time to think out their decisions than those who are more in line with your way of thinking.

How can you best avoid these mistakes?
When communicating with anyone, you have to have a clear understanding of the following:

You have to be aware of what their needs are for you to understand how and where to communicate with them. You need to know how and where they're coming from so that you can share with them in a way that motivates them.

When your mind and body are relaxed, there's no resistance between you and other people - they can know what you want and how you want it from the start. When your mind is relaxed and in control of your emotions, nothing is holding back anything that wants to come out.

You need to know yourself very well so that you can understand what you want from people and how to communicate with them so that they can know what you want from them because then there's no confusion between the two of you.

You have to be aware of your own emotions to understand how other people are feeling and what they're communicating - and this is where we need to be empathetic toward everyone. You have to have a clear understanding of your own needs to know what your needs are - and this is where we need to ensure our needs only serve others.

We have to be aware of the outcome we're trying to achieve for us to know what it is we want from people. The product has to benefit everyone. Otherwise, there's no point in talking with them about it.

You need to know how to communicate with people who are different from you because other people have different ways of thinking and feeling about things than you do. You have to be conscious of this difference when talking with them for them to feel free and open with you.

Now that we've listed the mistakes people make when talking with others, let's review some key points about what to do instead.

Here are two basic guidelines for communicating with others:

a) People have different needs from you. When communicating with them, we must be aware of how they're feeling and think to understand how they are in their own world so that we can be there for them where they need us to be.
b) If you're going to be talking with someone, you need a clear understanding of what it is you want from them. It would be best if you had a clearly defined goal to achieve and communicated with them in a way that inspires action on their part toward those goals.

The mistakes people make when communicating with others result from not knowing how people think and feel, not knowing what their needs are, not understanding the outcome you want from them, and not being able to communicate with other people in a way that motivates them.

To communicate with others effectively, you need knowledge about what they need from you and an understanding of how they're communicating with you so that you can respond appropriately. To avoid these mistakes, we need to be constantly aware of each of these things. If we never get to practice and develop our communication skills, it's going to be very difficult for us to communicate with other people in a way that produces results.

Chapter 8: How to Read People and Connect With Different Personality Types

Whether you are trying to make friends, improve your relationship, or get people to do what you want - knowing how different personality types work and how to talk with them will help you immensely. Knowing how different personality types work is only half of the story. Like the weather, there is no one-size-fits-all approach to conversation. Every conversation is a little different. Every person you talk to will be different and have their preferences. And this means that you must be able to read people and connect with them individually.

The first thing to understand about talking with people is that you are not just talking to them - you are communicating with them. Every person is different, so every conversation will play out differently. Most people don't realize it, but you can tell almost everything about a person simply by paying attention.

Remember that every word you say has a specific purpose (to move the conversation forward) and that every emotion, reaction, or movement a person makes will contribute to how the conversation plays out. If you can learn to read people and their patterns, you can predict better what they will do next and how they will react.

People are hardwired to think in patterns. Once you understand people's patterns, you can predict how they will react in any given situation. Knowing how people work is helpful for many situations in life, as it helps us understand what motivates them and why we should do things a certain way. If someone wants something from you and it is not beneficial for you to give it to them, a specific thought pattern will occur inside their head. Knowing these patterns can help you avoid situations that are not beneficial for you or others.

Learning to read people and connect with them will make you far more successful in life, business, relationships, and even social environments such as parties or networking events. It will open up your communication skills to a new level and allow you to be much more confident in any situation. You can overcome situations using your personality and abilities if you know how people think. There are many different personality types, but they all follow the same models. People repeatedly use the same thinking patterns and feel confident they are right. But the fact is that they often aren't. They follow practices that have worked in similar situations and often miss seeing other options that could work better.

For example, if you want to be more charming, you will find out quickly that being overly serious will not help you at all. You need to connect with people, relax around them and make them feel comfortable enough to open up to you without feeling threatened by you (which is something many more serious people fail at). If you are serious and try to come off as some kind of authority figure, or a person that is better than others, you will find that people will not like you very much. If you want to be more charming and likable, on the other hand, you need to come off as friendly, open-minded, and understanding. You need people to feel comfortable around you - maybe even a bit vulnerable - because this will make them open up to you.

These "moves" work in almost any situation where people need to connect. More severe and formal people often find it challenging to make friends with those who are not like them. They will try to be friends in the relationship and expect the other person to come around their way of thinking. The problem is that people have a hard time doing this, so they end up alone most of the time. If you can learn how personality types work, you will find many ways to communicate with others and build connections that benefit everyone involved.

People Problems

Personality types tend to conflict because we all want different things out of each situation. Many people out there want to fit in and be popular. Still, they tend to get along better with people who are more like them instead of those who are different. This can cause a whole lot of problems for those who are in their group, especially when the person ends up getting negative attention from those who are not in their group.

If your goal is to build relationships with groups of adults and younger people, it is good to find out how much you will clash with various personality types. For example, those who have a more severe personality will often fight with those whose characters are more laid-back and fun-loving. These differences will cause conflict because neither person is willing to change their side of the argument. For example, if you are a more serious person trying to build friendships with fun and outgoing people, you will often feel alienated. These people like to party, hang out and have a good time. On the other hand, you might be looking for something more serious and meaningful. You want to find someone to talk deeply about things with and connect with on a deeper level.

The other person might go along but be upset inside because they didn't see things the same way as you. The best thing you can do is try to understand that they see things differently from you so that they will react differently. This means that you need to act in a way that is consistent with how they see things so that they will be as comfortable with you as possible.

More serious people react negatively when others do not act as expected. This can happen when there is a disagreement between two groups of people, or it can be something that occurs between just two individuals. For example, if you are a more serious person and you start talking to someone fun-loving, they might not take you as seriously as you would like them to. This can make you feel isolated or that your concerns do not matter to the other person. This can also manifest itself in people being moody and unpredictable.

It would be best if you built a connection with the other person by connecting on their level - something often difficult for more serious people because they don't want to let go of the need for it all to make sense. In this case, you must stop behaving in a severe manner around them and begin acting as they would expect from someone who does not take things too seriously. However, if you can learn to recognize the differences in how people think, you will be able to connect with them on a deeper level, build a connection and have a lot more fun in your conversations.

This is one example of how people may act differently depending on who they are with. It is always essential to understand that others see things from their perspective, however much we might disagree with it. By understanding this basic fact about human nature and how personalities work, you will be able to build better connections with others so that everyone feels comfortable around each other.

There are ways to improve your conversational skills and get the person you are talking to comfortable:

1) Always be positive, even if you are criticizing

When you criticize someone, they will often feel defensive. They will not want to listen to what you say and will not be happy. Instead of attacking directly, try being positive and avoiding criticism. If you want someone to do something and they aren't doing it right or the right way, explain how you would like it done or suggest how you think it should be done. By doing so, the person you are talking with will have much less chance of feeling defensiveness and will be more likely to change their behavior to be closer to what you would like.

2) Build trust with everyone you talk to

Trust is a big part of communication. People are different, and so the way that you build trust with someone will be further from the person beside you. When talking to someone, try to find common ground or something that you both have in common. For example: If you are trying to get your partner to move into another apartment, try asking them about when they had to move and what made it difficult for them (common ground). People feel more comfortable when they can relate things in their past to things happening around them now. Building trust with people can simultaneously achieve more of what you want and what they want.

3) Take the time to listen to people

This one is a little harder. If you are trying to talk with someone, but they are not talking back, or they are talking about something that has nothing to do with you, ask the person what is in their mind. Listen and pay attention! This can be hard because, often, people do not want to be interrupted when they are talking. But by asking what is going on in their minds, you will learn a lot about them and be able to connect with them better.

4) Use core values/interests as a guide

When you know who someone is and where their interests lie, you will find it easier to understand their personality type and how they think. When you know this, you can use it to explain yourself and connect with them better. For example, if you are an artist and someone else knows, they will be more likely to listen to your advice and share their views. If you are talking with someone who shares the same interests, it is good to try connecting their interests with something important in your life now. When you connect people's core values with what is essential in your life, it helps them feel like they are more involved and interested in what is happening around them.

5) Use body language to your advantage

Keep track of everything you do with friends, family, and loved ones. Pay attention to how they sit, stand, or move and use this information. Often people will not notice when you are doing something slightly different (for example, not leaning on their desk as much), but over time this small thing will become more prominent. People have practiced sitting and standing in certain ways for years leading up to the specific situations they are in now. But what might be essential for them might not be very important for you and vice versa.

6) Understand the need for status

People want to feel important. Understanding this makes it easier to connect and become involved with others. For example, group members (such as team members, club members, or family) will want to feel like they are essential. They will want people to think that they are "in the know" and know what is happening in the group. People struggling socially and in life will often overcompensate by trying to impress others or create status by creating the illusion that they know more than they do. By understanding how groups (whether it be family members or friends) work, you can better distinguish whether someone is truly important or not.

7) Do not take things personally

Most people take things personally. They will see what you say (even if you realize that it is not a personal attack), and they will instantly begin to think about themselves, whether the thing you are talking about is good or bad for them. This can be highly frustrating for individuals who want to connect with others but cannot because of this. If people comment negatively on something that does not affect them, try to understand why they are saying it. You need to be able to find the reason behind their behavior; this will make it easier for you to connect with other people and increase your relationships.

Why People React Differently To Each Other

To communicate better with others, you need to understand their personalities. How someone sees the world is different from how another person sees it. This is caused by how people think; these differences affect their feelings. You can connect with people more personally and increase your relationships by understanding how people think. When you do this, you will understand people better and avoid the mistakes that most people make. You will also be able to express yourself and connect with others more effectively. By understanding other people's personalities, you can communicate with people better and build your relationships.

Human beings are hardwired to be sociable creatures. We all have specific patterns ingrained into us, so we can function in specific ways in a particular environment. However, it is not always easy to understand how people think or what motivates them when they make decisions and engage in situations they disagree with. By learning about these patterns, we can begin to understand people better and show them that our opinions matter. When we think about other people's needs before ourselves, our relationships become much more effective. We can also begin to read other people's body language and understand their motivations better. Paying attention to what people are doing and listening to what they have to say will help you connect with them and have a much more effective conversation.

Realize that all people are different, and we all have different ways of thinking about the world. Knowing how people feel is essential to understanding others, but it is not something that you should try too hard to develop or master. So, take a moment to discover what personality type you fall into and build connections with people based on that personality. The benefits of this are huge. Follow these tips on connecting with others, and you will improve your ability to communicate more effectively in any situation, regardless of your personality type.

Chapter 9: The Invisible Barriers Against Effective Communication and How to Address Them

It's hard to imagine how many barriers exist between two people in different places with different paths. They might be friends, colleagues, business partners, strangers on the street, etc., and they might want to talk to or even connect. Yet, there are always invisible barriers in the way, and then we wonder why it is so hard to secure. It's like two people who want to say something important but, for some reason, can't find a commonly spoken language. They might want to, but they don't know how. This book focuses on the communication barriers you face when you need to talk to someone at the moment and how to deal with them.

What are the barriers to effective communication?

There are many barriers to effective communication, yet there is one that stops most people from even trying to communicate. They cannot say what they want in a way others can hear or understand. It's like a linguistic disability that can be defined as communication anxiety. It's a feeling of vulnerability and uncertainty about approaching others, getting their attention, and then delivering the message for them to understand what you want.

You might think something wrong with your personality makes you anxious about communication, but this isn't true. If you have such feelings often, it's no surprise you struggle with communication daily. It's not you responsible for that feeling, but the way society has been built and conditioned. We live in a society where people are afraid to communicate directly and openly. That's why we use words so sparsely and often don't know how to say what we want to say clearly.

Some of the invisible barriers against effective communication include:

1. The tendency to lose your identity in the crowd: For example, someone addresses a large group simultaneously, and no one knows who they are talking about. It's easy for people to lose their identity when they communicate with many different people at once in the same room. People's identities (elements of themselves or personas) shift between interactions with other people, and therefore they have little chance of knowing what they want and implementing it. This can be a problem at work where people can't say what they want because they are afraid of conflict, looking bad, or being wrong. This deficiency in communication skills is likely to lead to problems.

2. **You are expected to take the initiative, and then you don't:** We have many situations like that, where you need to initiate a conversation or strike the first word, but you don't. For example, someone is sitting on a park bench alone reading a book, standing in line at the supermarket alone, or waiting at the bus stop alone. It might seem as if no one wants to engage in a conversation but think about it for a minute. Does it make sense? We are all social creatures who seek out interactions with others to grow as individuals. We are all pretty much the same. We all want to connect with others for 5 minutes or forever.

3. **You are afraid of revealing too much about yourself:** Sometimes, we are scared to reveal our true selves because it might be considered offensive. For example, we tell others who we are, what we want, and what motivates us. We are scared of being criticized, scolded, or judged by others. So instead of talking to somebody like a person, we usually try to hide our real intentions and thoughts about ourselves in order not to get rejected or hurt. We fear what people might think of us if they know our thoughts and intentions. It's easier to keep people at a distance by not being too honest and direct about ourselves. Instead, we are expected to present ourselves in less than our usual selves. When we do that, it's hard to form a connection with others.

4. We don't know how to be vulnerable: To admit your weakness and ask for help is the most important thing you can do when you want to connect with people you care about or regularly interact with. It's like the root of communication, the start of all communication. You can learn it from many places such as psychology, sociology, or even just observing other people, for example, when playing sports, playing guitar, or dancing. It's just that many people don't know how to use it helpful when talking to others. It's like our mother nature. We are all vulnerable from the moment we are born into this world and spend all our time learning how to be vulnerable, no matter our race, culture, or background.

5. Fear of conflict: This might be the most significant barrier to effective communication because people fear confrontation and argument. They want to say something but are afraid they won't find the right words, or they will get angry or even say something stupid in front of other people. Therefore, they prefer not to talk about important issues rather than say something wrong. That's why it is essential to include tactical communication skills in your communication toolkit.

6. The lack of confidence: People are afraid to speak up and share their opinion because they don't feel confident enough and think that what they say might not be suitable or interesting enough. They believe others will judge them if they say something wrong, stupid or irrelevant. That's why you need to know what makes people interested in your opinions and how you can deliver them in a way that people want to listen to and understand rather than criticize you.

7. Lack of interest: This is another barrier people face when trying to communicate with others. People don't want to talk about things that are not important or interesting enough, be it their problems, work problems, or anything else. This is why you need to learn how to remove barriers and make meaningful and valuable communication for others in your communication skills training.

What stops you from communicating effectively?

Our society has been built because we are taught to be shy and avoid conflict. It's not how we were brought up but how we have been conditioned into thinking. In some cases, fear can be used as a good sense of self-protection against potential risks. So instead of being open and honest with others, we prefer to stay quiet, and everyone will know what we want without having to tell them or say it out loud. In other situations, however, fear can be used against us to control our lives. Conflicts can be used as threats to keep us in a lower position in the hierarchy, in which case we are used to thinking we can't do anything about it but just take the punishment and suffer silently. If we don't get what we want because someone is blocking it, then that's a good time to start taking things into your own hands rather than being passive. We are just as good as anyone else, so you deserve to get what you want and need.

If we cannot be ourselves, there is no point in trying to connect with others. We are not the same people we were born with; we grow and change during our lifetime. Therefore, we must accept the person we have become and dwell within that person rather than trying to be someone else. The only way of communicating effectively is to be fully present in the moment and not worry about what other people might think of you. Why would you worry about that anyway? It would be best if you only cared about how well or poorly a conversation goes on with another human being.

The way you communicate makes you look at yourself and others differently. It's like a layer of glass standing between yourself and others, so you cannot perceive what is happening. Sometimes you need to look through that glass to see the accurate picture and understand how others see it.

The most important thing you can learn in communication is how to listen to other people, not just for understanding but for the ability to communicate with them. Does this sound too simple? It's like understanding yourself better. You can only understand others if you can understand yourself first. So when you say things out loud, you need to be aware of what you are saying by noticing your behavior, body language and words, and other people's emotions. Otherwise, you won't be able to achieve what you set out for in your communication training.

How do you overcome the invisible barriers against effective communication?

This is the only question we will focus on in this book because it's the most fundamental problem people face when they try to communicate with others. No magic pill you can take will automatically remove the barriers and make you an effective communicator. Communication is something you learn and practice over and over again. The good news is that once you know how to communicate effectively, it will stay with you forever, and you will use your communication skills daily.

You will also be able to improve your communication skills by learning how to overcome the barriers that block and prevent effective communication.

Here are tips on how to overcome the invisible barriers to effective communication:

How do we overcome problems in communication?

First of all, you need to learn how other people communicate. If you are interested in someone else, the chances are you will become good friends if you can understand them, what makes them tick and what motivates them. Why is that so? It's because understanding someone else helps build trust between two people. The more faith there is between two people, the easier it will be for two people to connect and form a meaningful relationship or, in other words, a friendship that lasts forever.

1. Tune into your own emotions: If you don't know how you feel, how can you expect to read the feelings of others? It's essential to be self-aware and learn how to communicate with yourself calmly so you can then communicate with other people calmly.

2. Be present in the moment: You cannot communicate effectively if your mind is elsewhere. You need to be fully there and focus on what's happening, who's around, and what they are saying so that you can respond to their needs rather than your own. This also applies when you talk on the phone or speak face-to-face with someone.
3. Don't be afraid to ask questions: To understand someone, you need to know what they want, which means asking them. This can be awkward and difficult at first, but it's an absolute must for effective communication. You need to make sure that you listen thoroughly, are interested in what the other person has to say, and don't rush through the conversation so you can get away from uncomfortable situations or people as quickly as possible.
4. Confidence is critical: Confidence is part of how people communicate, interact with others, and feel about themselves in life. Your communication skills training will show if you don't feel confident about yourself. If you are optimistic, others will instantly be attracted to you and want to talk with you. It's essential to put yourself out there and start being more spontaneous. The more confident and relaxed you become, your communication skills training will be more effective.
5. Be aware of what you want to talk about: Before you start the conversation, think about what the other person has to say and what you would like to ask them. If you don't know what to say, see if you can come up with an idea before starting a conversation. Also, try to learn more about the person from their words and body language before speaking to understand that person better.

6. Accepting your emotions: One of the best ways to improve communication is to start accepting yourself. This means being in a good mood, buying all your feelings, and knowing you are good enough to communicate with others.
7. Don't let fear block you: If someone is blocking you from achieving something you want, let go of the fear so you can move forward and complete it yourself. Get rid of everything that stands in your way, learn how to manage life situations on your own, and manage things so that they work out for the better.
8. Learn to listen: It's not just important to hear what people say; learning how to listen makes others feel better because they feel you care. You will also be able to communicate with them more effectively if you show that you are listening.
9. Don't take things personally: If someone is angry or upset, they haven't done it just because of you. People have their own lives and problems, so don't blame yourself for being unable to fix them or solve the problem for them. Take things as they are and work on improving your communication skills training.
10. Flexibility is vital: If people want to communicate in a certain way, you should go along with it. If the other person wants to be more serious, then do that. If the other person wants to lighten the mood and be happy, follow suit and become satisfied. It's all about being flexible.

Communication is about being transparent, open, and honest with each other. Invisible communication barriers can be compared to blocks that prevent people from connecting, communicating, and working together. These barriers are hidden, but they are very much there. If you want to communicate effectively with others, try to eliminate the barriers to communication by listening, understanding, and respecting others. You will see the results of your communication skills training. Also, keep in mind the tips that have been mentioned in this book on how to overcome invisible communication barriers. This will help you communicate better with others and in life and develop a better personal relationship with yourself.

Chapter 10: Secrets to Becoming an Empathetic Listener and Conversationalist

If you have difficulties establishing and maintaining relationships within any circle, the lack of communication skills is probably one of the reasons. It is essential to effectively communicate your thoughts and ideas, not only to you but also to other people. Speaking skills are the starting point of any relationship. From a young age, we are all taught that communication is essential and it is something that you will always have with you. The problem, however, with many people is that they forget how important and valuable it can be to them and others, especially when they are in a relationship with another person or even someone at work.

Communication is something that you're always supposed to be able to achieve. Whether you are talking to your friends, family members, a girlfriend or boyfriend, or even when it comes to communicating at work or school, communication is essential, and something that you should always be able to have with every single person in your life, why do we forget about it and why do we have issues when it comes to relationships? Many of us are too afraid of hurting the other person's feelings or becoming awkward in some way by not being able to communicate well with the people we love or even with those we work with.

So if communication is essential for every aspect of your life, why do so many people forget about it and let relationships fall apart because they cannot communicate? The answer to this question is quite simple—we all want to be liked and accepted by everyone. We want everyone to get and love us just the way we are, with no faults and imperfections. We need to be taken by others to feel safe and secure. However, we also tend to be too judgmental towards people around us. Many of us tend to forget that everyone is different from one another, whether it's their personality or simply the way they look at life.

Because we want people to like us for who we are and don't want them to point out our faults or imperfections, we forget how essential communication skills can be for our relationships. We want to be like everyone else, and by communicating with others, we can better understand them and get to know them on a more personal level. By communicating well with someone, we can tell them about ourselves, let them tell us about themselves, and learn more about that particular person. If we don't communicate well with someone and don't take the time to listen, we will never really know who they are or what they think or feel. And if we don't know someone very well, then they will be just another person to us. We will see them as strangers, cats, or dogs. Someone we don't know and someone who doesn't matter to us.

Communication is the starting point for every relationship that you might have in your life. We need to be able to listen and talk with people for relationships to work with each other. If you are unable to communicate well with someone, then you won't be able to understand them, and that relationship won't last very long at all.

From the time we learn to speak, we also know how to listen; but in some cases, this does not seem to be taught or practiced enough. Most people listen to what others say, but rarely can they make sense of the conversation, let alone respond appropriately. In a relationship, this lack of empathy and ability to be understanding is seen as a sign of disrespect. It is often considered when deciding whether you can be in a relationship with someone.

So what are the secrets to becoming an empathetic listener and conversationalist?

1. Commit to listen

Listen to others. Sometimes you want others to listen to what you have to say, but these people may not be able to pay attention to what you're saying. If this is the case, then use this time as an opportunity to learn from them. Listen and learn from their experiences because, in a way, they are also teaching you how not to have the same life as theirs. It's about giving and receiving; nothing is without effort, so giving worth listening to will give you some suitable lessons.

2. Always have a genuine interest in what others say

Genuine interest doesn't always mean you agree with their perspective, but it does mean that you are open to listening and learning from them. If you don't seem genuinely interested in what they have to say, they will feel ignored and frustrated with you.

3. Show interest by asking questions

Ask questions if you or someone else is expressing a point of view. A good way of asking questions is to keep the exchange from becoming one-sided by asking for further information about what the other person is saying. The more specific your question is, the more likely you'll get an answer, and that answer should lead to another question where possible.

4. Make sure you are giving them your full attention

If you are busy and in a hurry, don't ask the other person to listen to what you have to say. You have to lead by example regarding things like empathy and listening. People will not only learn communication skills from you, but they'll also pick up on your attitude. You can't expect others to attend if you are never willing or able to give the same respect in return.

5. Don't make assumptions about what you hear

You must be very careful when making assumptions about what you hear. We tend to believe that the first words out of someone's mouth are always accurate. This is not always the case because people don't always communicate as they want. When you listen, ask questions, and remember that people always try to tell you something. Sometimes they may have a point different from your own, but they will still reach an agreement or a compromise with the other person if they see that it is worth persevering with.

6. Don't interrupt

The art of listening is unique; sometimes, it requires you to be patient with the speaker. If they choose to speak, continue to listen; you cannot make it your business to speed things up or hurry them along. You must listen with your full attention and

allow others to talk or express themselves. The essential part of communication is hearing the other person, not only what they are saying but also their feelings at that particular time.

7. Don't make judgments

The art of listening is a potent tool to have. It can help you to understand someone's perspective and get insight into their message. The problem is that when people are bent on making judgments, they often miss the point the speaker is trying to convey. The art of listening requires you to show genuine interest in what others have to say, regardless of whether or not you agree with it or would like them to say something more specific. Judgments are made because we feel we can do things better than others. The art of listening allows you to open yourself up to a different perspective, which you may find surprising or even enlightening.

8. Give people feedback

The art of good communication is simply being able to hear not only what someone says but also hearing them. Don't be afraid to tell the other person what you think about what they say. If it is positive, compliment them. If it is negative, let them know. If a person is telling you that they cannot receive information from someone else in a certain way, let them know; this will allow you to find ways for this problem to be resolved and perhaps resolve it before it even comes up.

Communication is a powerful thing. It can provide us with some fantastic opportunities and experiences. Communication works both ways; you will find that whatever you put into the universe, positive or negative, will always come back to you. The same goes for communication; if you want to be someone others trust and feel comfortable telling about their problems or life experiences, you have to do the same for them when they open up to you. If we send out specific signals or clues that we are unwilling to listen to, people will close themselves off us. This means they will stop sharing their ideas and feelings with us because they feel they cannot trust us enough to listen without judgment or interruption. It is not always easy to be a good listener, but it can be one of the most rewarding things that you ever learn to do. Don't waste your chance and learn to listen more, for it will make all the difference in your relationships.

Being an empathetic listener means listening to the intent and message of the other person. It means being respectful in what you say, your voice, and your facial expressions. It also means focusing on the person's needs, wants, desires, and goals. A good listener is available to take in what they have to say, ask questions when necessary and let them know that you are interested in hearing from them. They will feel accepted, valued, and seen by the other person. Being an empathetic listener is not just about words but about showing people that you care for them personally and professionally.

It takes time and effort to be a good listener. It is not something that can easily be accomplished overnight. The art of listening is not just about hearing another person's words but also about hearing the intention behind those words. Good listeners will take their time to understand what the other person is trying to tell them. They make sure they truly understand the message, no matter how difficult or uncomfortable it may seem at first. It doesn't matter how long it takes to comprehend what someone is trying to say fully; they will do whatever they need to understand the message correctly.

Being an empathetic listener means putting the other person first. It doesn't matter what the other person is saying or how they are saying it. All that matters is that their needs and desires are being met. Their feelings are more important than your own; it doesn't matter what you want, as long as you can help them to get what they need. The art of listening requires a willingness to accept someone else for who they are, faults and all, without judging who they should be or should have been in the past.

A good listener is open and non-judgmental to all communication from others. They don't jump to conclusions and try to remain calm and relaxed when communicating. They don't judge what others say or how they say it. They take in other people's feelings and thoughts without being defensive or hurt. A good listener is interested in learning what another person has to say, who they are, and their hopes, dreams, aspirations, and goals.

Patience and understanding of human nature are part of the art of listening. It takes time to develop the ability to listen well. The art of listening requires a willingness to give your full attention to the person you are talking with. It means learning how their mind works, taking in what they have just said, and seeing all the emotions that may be guiding them in their actions and expressing themselves. It also means being able to listen to unspoken messages as well as what is being said.

It takes two people for communication to work. However, it does not mean you will automatically be a good listener. You will need someone willing to let you know what they want and allow you to understand where their thoughts and feelings are coming from. A person that can give you feedback so that you can learn what they think and feel when it comes down to communicating with others. It would be best if you had someone who has confidence in your ability so that they can fully express themselves without worrying about being misunderstood or misinterpreted by others. A good listener makes sure the other person understands what they are trying to say, even if it is difficult or painful for them. They give their honesty and genuine concerns so that they know they care and it is not a waste of their time when talking to them. This also shows they want to understand who they are as an individual. A good listener is willing to listen to what the other person has to say and how they say it and ask for clarification when necessary.

Being a good listener means listening and finding out what the other person wants and needs from you. It means understanding their goals as well as giving them the ability to express themselves and their feelings. It also means being aware of what the other person is feeling. They are not just reacting out of fear or anger; there may be more. They feel something else but aren't sure what they are doing, thinking, and feeling at that moment. A good listener will discover this to understand better and support their partner no matter what is causing them discomfort or pain in their lives.

Chapter 11: How to Form Your Message to Get Your Point Across Effectively

Have you ever been confused about how to start a conversation with someone? If you have, you've probably missed out on potentially great discussions. Imagine that you want to talk to someone, and they are not giving you eye contact or seem disinterested in talking. You might feel unwelcome and think it is difficult for them to stand there and listen to your story. Or you might be talking to an individual and wonder if you should tell them about the latest movie or book you just read.

Think about a time when someone didn't give you eye contact or when their responses seemed slow. What was their response to your comments? Was their body language helpful? If not, how did they respond?

Remember how they responded, and then use this knowledge in future conversations to help you maintain a relationship with that person. The next time a good friend or family member comes up to talk to you, consider what approach worked best for that person in your current situation. Did you make an interesting comment? Did you tell them a joke? How could you improve your approach and make their next visit more fun or meaningful?

What are some common mistakes people make while communicating with other people? What do some people do in their conversations that help to drive away listeners or create an awkward situation?

We all experience communication problems at some point in our lives. Even if we have developed excellent communication skills, sometimes people will not always understand us the way we want them to. Communication is a two-way street, so we must ensure that both parties understand one another.

Here are some helpful tips on how to form your message to get your point across effectively:

1) Ask for clarification if you want a second chance at conveying your point: The first thing that comes to mind when thinking of asking someone for clarification is a student who asks their teacher the same question repeatedly. It doesn't matter how often you ask this person; they will not remember what you said or how to answer your questions. Even if you are talking about something simple like "When did Ike become president?" and ask them several times for clarification, they might still have no idea what happened.
2) Stick with one topic: When in a conversation, sit back, relax and listen to the other person's responses. Do they respond to your comments with enthusiasm? If so, you're in a good spot. Don't press the matter if their body language is unfriendly, defensive, or uninterested. The more you try to get their attention and demand your point, the less receptive they will be to what you are saying.
3) Let them know what you want from them: "I want to talk to you about something that can make a big difference in our lives." This shows your listener that you have at least one topic in mind and asks for their input. It also lets them know that it is essential to you.

4) Listen to the other person: People who value conversation will find a way to make all the people they talk to feel comfortable. Pay attention to their words if you are interested in what they say. If you are only concerned with getting your points across, it will be challenging to know what they want or how their thoughts might influence yours. This can ruin a good relationship because friends and family don't like feeling that their space is being invaded by someone else and are pushing for you to go away.
5) Know how to say "no" (without coming across as rude): Learn how to say "no" as soon as you realize that the topic might not be exciting or pertinent for the circumstances and people around you. The purpose of saying "no" is to let them know it is not a good time for that topic and help them to move on with something that might work better.
6) Prepare what you want to say: What can you say that will be meaningful and engaging? You might not even get what you wanted to say out in the first place. It is best to have a few prepared lines or ideas before you start to speak. If you have nothing prepared, then you can easily fall into a meandering conversation that lasts longer than it should.
7) Know when to pause and let the other person talk: You might want to respond to what the other person says, but you are obligated to listen first. Sometimes this means you need a little bit of time so that you can form your thoughts and comments. Don't be in a hurry when it comes to starting your thoughts. Give yourself as much time as necessary, especially if the other person is talking fast or it seems like they are rushing through their words.

8) Avoid interrupting: The simple rule is that if someone's comments are confusing you or seem out of place, let them have a chance to present their thoughts before you jump in with your questions or comments. People appreciate it when someone takes their time to think about what they want to say, has patience, and tries not to interrupt them when they say something important.
9) Take notice of how you say something: There are two parts to the message you are sending. The first part is what you're saying, and the second is how you say it. This can mean your body language and tone of voice. You want to ensure that what you say matches up with your tone of voice or body language. If someone seems upset, ensure that your message matches the style of their voice or body language style. If someone seems happy, ensure your message matches their facial expressions and overall mood.
10) Maintain eye contact: Often, people will not speak with us unless we maintain eye contact. They might even tell us to look away if they are uncomfortable looking at someone. When trying to convey something to another person, there is no need to avoid their gaze and stare at the ground or the middle of their face. Stay focused on their eyes and maintain an appropriate level of eye contact.
11) Be truthful: You cannot be dishonest and expect a good result from your conversation. If you lie, it will likely come across in your voice tone or body language, making the person feel more uneasy with you than if you were honest from the start. Honest and open communication is the best way to maintain a good relationship with others.

12) Avoid being judgmental: No one wants to be judged by their opinions, thoughts, and feelings. If you think someone is wrong or their view is too romantic, it is best to think about how you want to respond. The best way of responding could be just saying, "I understand where you are coming from, but I want to let you know that I disagree." You could also say, "I disagree with that thought because of this reason. " Try not to judge what they say or paraphrase what they believe in a way they find offensive. If you can't do this, it will be better to keep your thoughts to yourself and not get into a long, drawn-out explanation of why they are wrong.
13) Use the person's name: This shows that you have an interest in who they are as a person. You can also use their name in your comments or responses to let them know you are paying attention to what they are saying. You don't have to say their word in every other sentence, but make sure you throw in some references that respect the other person's identity.
14) Avoid multitasking when you are in a conversation: Be present and focused on the other person. You might have stuff going on in your life, but you have to set them aside for the time being to have an intimate and meaningful relationship with the person you are speaking to. If you choose to act like there is something more important than talking to someone, don't be surprised if they seem upset or offended by what you are saying. They don't let these things slide because they want a good relationship with somebody who cares about them.

Getting your point across effectively can be tough every time you try. There are some instances where you might have to say the same thing repeatedly to get your point across. If you can learn how to do this effectively, it could mean that people might start noticing who you are and what you have to say. You could become a compelling individual because of how you communicate with others.

When speaking, try to find ways to make your communication more personal and meaningful by being truthful and exhibiting integrity at every opportunity. You want everyone to know that you care about them as a person and not just as an object used for your gain or pleasure unless it is part of a consensual relationship.

As you get older and deal with more people, you might learn that being an effective communicator will help ensure you live a fulfilling life and have a good relationship with others. You don't have to be an eloquent speaker to be able to say what needs to be said effectively.

It will take time, but if you are persistent and patient, you can learn how to become an effective communicator. You'll be surprised by the amount of positive feedback from communicating effectively. When other people see this happening, they will want to get involved in communication because they see how fruitful it is for your social relationships.

With communication, you must be open to feedback, criticism, and the possibility of being wrong. You will be wrong sometimes, but that doesn't mean that your alternative perspectives aren't valid. It would be best to consider other options before deciding what's more sensible or plausible.

When you are open to a good conversation and willing to respect the other person's point of view, they are likely to listen and believe what you have to say. They might not always agree with your point of view, but they will at least listen intently so as not to miss anything important that you might say.

The more you learn to be a good communicator, the more people will say positive things about you. Effective communication allows you to stand out from the crowd and attract people by demonstrating your commitment to being an effective communicator.

As an effective communicator, you are someone that other people can depend on because they know you are trustworthy and reliable. You can help others when they need it most because they can be assured that you will listen intently and provide what is required. They know your advice is worth considering, even if it isn't always followed. The other person will probably feel that whatever you say is important enough to understand and listen to.

As you become a more effective communicator, new relationships can blossom and grow in your life. Your friends, family, and acquaintances will notice your growth in this area and see you as someone they can be comfortable being around. You'll have a way of communicating that encourages others to be open with you, which means you are more likely to be motivated and inspired daily.

Finding out how important effective communication is in a relationship might make you want to do things differently. You will get your point across effectively so that the other person knows that you are sincere and have their best interest in mind. You will be interested in learning how they are doing daily and be mean to make sure they know you care about them as more than just a friend or acquaintance. When you learn how to be an effective communicator, it will open up whole new horizons for you. You'll be able to focus on having meaningful and intimate relationships with the people around you. You'll also know that whenever you want to talk about something important, someone will be willing to listen intently and show their support for what is being said. With effective communication, you can create an atmosphere where others can hear what you have to say and take it into account when making decisions. You'll find that others will come to you when they want a thoughtful perspective on a situation, so make sure you are always ready to give your two cents. If all else fails, keep telling them the same thing differently until they understand what you are trying to say.

Chapter 12: The Art of Conveying Your Thoughts and Feelings Across Different Mediums

Have you ever found yourself in a scenario where you've been told to do something but don't know how and find it extremely difficult to communicate that fact? The person you're speaking to isn't making it easy on themselves, either. Perhaps they feel the same way that they aren't being heard or might be in a situation where they don't want their feelings hurt.

Well, it's no surprise that communication skills are so integral - our jobs rely on us being able to articulate ideas clearly and concisely. Yet it's astonishing how many of us don't know how best to do this. Understanding another person's tone of voice and body language is essential to convey your message. When we have a conversation, our tone, choice of words, and body language can tell the other person whether we're being friendly or hostile towards them.

Communicating your thoughts and feelings across different mediums, especially during a conversation, is extremely important, but there are two parts you need to get right:

First, you need to read the person you're speaking to and ensure they're in an excellent mental and emotional place to talk. We do this by observing their body language and tone of voice. This will give the impression that you care about the other person's well-being.

Your tone of voice is vital for communication consistency with what you're saying. If you're speaking in a monotone voice or sounding disinterested, the other person will get bored or not take you seriously.

Secondly, as you begin to talk about this issue/topic, think about what the other person needs to hear and how you can show them by example. The best way to do this is through stories. When we tell stories, we use words that excite our emotions and paint a picture in others' minds. Most of us don't like to be told that we're boring or that our stories are boring, so it's essential to paint a picture and give examples that will make your story interesting.

Many people are afraid to talk in groups because they think they're not good enough or will say the wrong thing. Once you understand your communication skills, you won't have to worry about this! If you feel uncomfortable talking in front of a group, try practicing in front of a mirror or with friends and family. You can start practicing on others when you get used to it and feel more confident. Remember that if you want people to listen to your opinion/proposal, make sure it's short and snappy. Don't beat around the bush - get straight to the point.

If you're in the middle of a conversation and feel like you're not being listened to, stop speaking, look away from the other person, and think about how you can be more direct. This will make your message more understandable for them.

This will only work if it's done respectfully. If you've rolled your eyes or scoffed at what they've said, they'll take it as a sign that you don't care or that they should take a break so their feelings won't hurt. Remember, you're initiating the conversation, and it's not your job to correct people constantly. If you're trying to convince someone of something, then you have a responsibility to get them on board with what you're saying.

Another way you can improve your communication skills is to see if the other person is getting bored. If they are, repeat what they've said using different words or tell them how you feel about it. People will see that you're taking an interest, and they'll be more inclined to talk in the future.

Topics with acronyms will be complex for people who don't know the subject. It's advisable to draw on your experiences to do what you do. If you're trying to convey something but using a lot of adjectives, the message will be lost, as the words don't relate to each other.

You must be honest and genuine when communicating with others - people have a sixth sense for telling when someone is being fake, which often makes them feel uncomfortable about talking to that person again. This can cause problems for your relationship if they misinterpret it (they'll think that you don't like them or that they didn't speak as much).

Another way to look at communication skills is that everyone makes mistakes, and we always learn. It's essential to learn from your mistakes and find new ways of communicating with others that work for you.

If you're having difficulty communicating with someone, try not to judge them harshly. Don't think badly of them or put yourself in the other person's shoes if they use inappropriate words or act aggressively toward you. Many people who have had difficult childhoods suffer from depression and low self-esteem - these are just some of the many mental health problems that can make it hard for a person to communicate effectively.

Perhaps the other person is under a lot of stress and feels like you do not understand them - this could be due to their way of communicating with others. If you don't know how to communicate with someone in your life, then take the time to educate yourself about what they're experiencing. This will help you learn how to communicate effectively with that person, so they feel better about sharing their thoughts and feelings.

To communicate effectively, we should first listen. By listening, we can give the other person our full attention and not let our thoughts cloud our judgment or interrupt what they say. They need to know that when they speak to you, you're taking an interest in what they have to say. To do this, repeat and summarize what the other person has said and see if this makes sense.

It's also important to compliment or express how we feel in the conversation so that the other person knows we're interested in them. If they're not being listened to and feel like nobody else is there for them, they won't discuss their feelings with others again.

You can also look at another person's face while talking - this will show that you're interested in what they have to say and will demonstrate your body language. Now practice these techniques, and you'll find that your conversations will become much more effective, and you'll be able to communicate with others in a way they'll understand.

Problems with communication are a common cause of arguments and conflict, but importantly they're also an opportunity for us to learn how to communicate better. When people don't like our ideas, new points of view, or what we have to say, it's essential not to show annoyance, anger, or irritation. Remember that most people won't get angry if you explain your position clearly and show them why it's the best course of action for them.

We can show someone we're interested in what they're saying by repeating what we've heard, paraphrasing, and summarizing their point of view. By looking at their face and body language when they're talking to us, we'll get a better idea of how they feel. If they're frowning or offering gestures, we should get in touch with them to see if something is wrong or ask why they are unhappy instead of ignoring it.

When someone says something difficult for us to hear or understand, then try not to react like this comes as a surprise because they may misinterpret our reaction if we do.

We should also be courteous when questioning a person's point of view, even if we disagree. This can help us see that they are serious about their position so we can take them seriously.

If someone is pushing to make an argument, we shouldn't fight with them but use our words to express the facts and let them know our reasons for disagreeing with them. When people are too hasty in making their point of view known, they may not have put enough thought into it. Before persuading them otherwise, we must understand why they feel strongly about the topic.

If someone is too aggressive towards us when we disagree with their ideas, we should try to deal with them rationally. By showing them that you're not willing to fight with them, you'll be able to get your message across without getting into a physical conflict. Understandably, they'll feel annoyed or hostile if they feel like they've been insulted, but this doesn't mean that you have to argue back at them or be dismissive of their feelings.

The goal of communication isn't just to express our ideas effectively and persuade the other person - it's also about working together as a team. We may not see eye to eye on every subject, but we can be united in believing that what we have to say is best for the greater good.

The essential part of communication is being transparent, honest, and genuine. If you appear to lack confidence at first, don't panic. It's better to start communicating effectively if this is not your forte than to hold back and leave someone confused about why you're being unresponsive.

Before communicating with someone else, prepare to demonstrate how much you care about them and your ideas. To be a more effective communicator, you'll need to think about what people are saying while listening to them. Pay attention to their intonation, tone, and facial expression - these will help you understand what the other person is saying.

If you listen well, you'll make it easier for the other person to talk to us and show us how they feel. We should put ourselves in the shoes of the other person we're communicating with to see how they're feeling.

When we listen carefully, we won't find it as hard to express our ideas or add something of value that nobody else can say - because when we listen well, we hear what they're going through.

What good reasons do you have NOT to communicate with someone?
Sometimes we can feel reluctant to talk to others, but this isn't necessarily bad. We should only speak to the people that want to hear what we have to say, and if we don't see this as necessary, then it doesn't matter if somebody else does.

For instance, we may feel that the people around us are not listening well enough. When they speak, they may not seem interested in what we have to say, or they may interrupt us during our conversations. If this is the case, we should keep our distance from them because they'll distract us from what we're trying to focus on.

There are other reasons why we shouldn't communicate with someone, like if we have no common interests with them or if it doesn't fit with the way that we want to live our lives. If we feel nervous when talking to someone because they're too aggressive, it might not be worth speaking with them whenever they want to talk to us.

Whatever the reason is not to communicate with someone, most of the time, it's better not to deal with them.

By looking at how other people communicate, you can learn how to do it yourself more effectively. If you want to influence someone positively, then it's essential to understand how you can get better at doing so.

By observing a person's behavior, you'll see what seems to interest them and what they're passionate about. You may also be able to see when they're having a difficult time in their life, but you can show that you care by asking them how they're doing or helping them in some way.

We can take lessons from other people as long as we're careful not to copy or imitate them - because this may land us in trouble. We should pay attention to the words and body language of someone else so we can use our own to communicate effectively with others.

Several resources are available to help us communicate well with others. Another way that we can gain insight into how to communicate well is by reading stories, studies, and books about famous writers and public speakers. By analyzing their behaviors and saying things the way they have, we can expand our vocabulary and become more expressive.

When we're ready to talk to someone else, our body language must be open so that the person isn't distracted from what we're trying to say. If we feel nervous, we should stand up straight and smile so that it won't make people uncomfortable.

We may not feel confident in how we speak about our ideas and influences, but that doesn't mean we can't change it for the better. It's easy to get distracted by other people or our thoughts, but if someone tries to explain something to us clearly, we should be open to listening.

If you're uncomfortable with how you speak, then you should talk to other people and try to engage them in conversation. By talking to others, we can learn how they express their ideas and respond when we talk back - so we must spend time talking with others so they can give us feedback on how effective our communication is.

When we're in conversation with someone else, we need to try and listen to what they have to say as much as they do. This can be challenging because we might feel they're not interested in what we have to say or are talking over us - especially if this is the case. By observing others, we can improve our relationships with others.

If our communication skills are unclear, then we shouldn't bother trying to talk about an issue because this may leave people confused. We should encourage these people so that they'll help us improve how we communicate our ideas and influences.

We can't change something we're not confident with, but we can be open to feedback from others to get encouragement. The best way to do this is by asking what people think about our ideas, but sometimes we should listen and ask if they have any advice or tips on how we should express ourselves.

If people around us don't want to talk, then it's probably better for us not to bother. It doesn't matter what these people say - all that matters is that they won't help us in any way and will distract us from what we need to focus on.

Here are some things we can do that can help us better understand and portray our thoughts and feelings during a conversation:

1. Formulate your thoughts. Come up with a list of areas you need to address and how exactly you will do so. Your friend or co-worker might feel the same, but they won't always know how they should be able to convey that to you, which is why it's your responsibility to ask them some questions.
2. Be aware of the situation. Are you in a position where your friend or co-worker might feel uncomfortable about what you're about to say? Are there other people around? Let them know that, no matter what, they shouldn't feel judged and that sometimes it's just easier if we can talk without others around us knowing our issues.
3. Don't get frustrated. If you find that your friend or co-worker isn't as forthcoming with their thoughts as you'd like them to be, try not to get frustrated at them. It's just not a great way to start a conversation.
4. Don't be afraid of confrontation. If someone is coming around and talking down to you or others, stand up for yourself and others! Please make your voice heard when necessary; it's better than pretending everything is okay when it isn't!

5. Take some responsibility for the other party's feelings. If a friend or family member complains about you to you, it's not their fault that they have problems communicating. Try to make them realize that communication is an essential skill, and try not to get too frustrated because they need some time to think of how they will handle things.
6. Be the bigger person. If someone gets upset and suddenly calls you names in an argument, don't take things too personally - it's tough when you receive hurtful remarks like this from a family member or friend that we're close with. Try saying something positive or polite to them after your argument has ended.
7. Listen carefully. If you are conversing with someone and ask them a question they've asked you to address but don't fully understand, then repeat it to them so that they know what you're trying to understand.
8. Make eye contact when speaking. It makes us feel confident and puts us in control of the conversation, which we think might usually make us blurt out our thoughts before we have time to process them properly.
9. Be specific. Don't make generalizations - if something is bothering your friend or family member, then tell them precisely what bothers you so that they can get directed towards the right place to find the source of their disagreement or upset with themselves.
10. Listen attentively. If someone is having a conversation with you and you have no clue how to respond again, listen intently for a couple of seconds before answering them. We feel it's best not to interrupt an individual when speaking to us, especially if what they say isn't much help.

Conveying your thoughts and feelings across different mediums is essential in our everyday lives as we seek to do well in everything we do. It enables us to give off the right impression and effectively express our emotions, opinions, and ideas, stay in touch with others and keep them updated with what's happening in our lives. The art of public speaking helps us to talk about our opinions in front of other people without getting tongue-tied. We rely on communication skills daily, and many problems can occur if we don't use them correctly. This can affect our personal and professional lives, and we often find ourselves unable to communicate effectively in certain situations.

Communication is an essential skill we all need to learn, whether agitated or lethargic, as it helps us feel comfortable in any situation. There are many types of communication skills training: you can know how to translate a written report into a formal letter; you can also take part in body language training, where you can gauge how other people react when you make specific movements. However, the most effective way of improving your communication skills is through the written word. Here are some things anyone can do to enhance their communication skills.

Formulate your thoughts. No matter the topic, you will find that you don't always understand what you hear. This is because there are two sides to every conversation; we must know what they mean when we listen to someone talking to us. By coming up with a list of points or issues you have with yourself or your life, then put these down on paper so that you can read them back later when you feel uncomfortable and need help. This cannot be easy at first, but it is the best way to ensure you take an optimistic life approach.

When you are having a conversation, make sure that you understand what the other party is saying to you before opening your mouth and answering. This way, you won't come across as ignorant or unintelligent and can feel comfortable speaking with those around you.

When it comes to what to say, try to be more tactful when communicating your feelings. If someone has upset you, don't pause for a second before telling them this, as this will allow them time to prepare a counterargument. It's always best to try and say something to make the other party feel better about themselves and then move forward.

When we learn new skills, it helps us to become even more confident than before. One thing that anyone can do to help improve their communication skills is to share them with others. The next time you're conversing with someone, have them write down what they think the other party is trying to get across. Then, ask them a question to clarify what they mean. This will allow you to practice your skills in front of others and help you feel more productive when communicating with others around you.

Chapter 13: How to Give Useful Feedback Without Offending People

When giving feedback to someone, you want to be constructive; yet your feedback can often come across as negative and even hurtful. It's easy to assume that people will react negatively, but it helps to remember that we all have different perceptions and reactions.

Here are some tips on how you can get the most sensitive feedback from the other person in your conversation:

1. Be specific

Use specific examples as much as possible; this will help them understand what they do that causes particular problems or makes certain outcomes happen. The more detailed and specific you can be, the less likely your feedback will be misunderstood. For example, instead of saying, "You are a sloppy worker," try, "You get distracted by listening to your radio when you work." If you don't know enough details about what or how the person does something, don't bother giving them feedback. It's not worth it.

2. Use I-messages

Avoid using you-messages when giving feedback. Instead of "You are a sloppy worker," try "I feel frustrated when I see your work piled up on your desk." Also, consider the other person's response if they received the same feedback. If they made excuses or became defensive, don't say it. You want to say things in a way that won't cause this reaction.

3. Make the feedback specific and non-judgmental

Focus on how something was done instead of why it was done (unless you know the reason is related to a personal value). For example, instead of saying, "Your work is sloppy," try, "I had trouble understanding your report. I think it can be more clearly written." The second statement focuses on how the work was done rather than why it was done. The less judgmental you are, the more likely people will listen to what you say.

4. Ask for clarification

If something isn't clear, ask for more details and examples before giving feedback. This shows that you're interested in understanding them (rather than just dumping on them).

5. State your observations and feelings about the incident in question

Be honest and discuss your thoughts on the incident if you give feedback. State what worked well and what could be improved. It helps to compare this to similar situations that have occurred in the past, but that isn't always possible. If it is difficult for you to talk openly about these things without being judgmental, don't feel wrong about verbalizing it in any way that makes sense.

6. Try not to react in anger

It's very tempting when someone does something that bothers or frustrates us to assume they did it with malicious intent wrongly. Try to be calm and ahead of the situation by asking yourself, "What is this person really thinking or feeling instead of assuming the worst?"

When someone's behavior or attitude bothers you, it can be easy to think about how it reflects on you. If you are standing in front of your boss complaining that the kitchen needs cleaning, some people might think he's talking about your work habits. You might think he's attacking you if you start to get angry.

When others are critical of behavior, they can often be required of your heart and mind. They may have difficulty accepting that the person they're talking to could also be doing their work poorly or taking criticism wrongly.

7. Don't be defensive

When you're defensive, it makes others feel uncomfortable and uneasy. When you're defensive, you focus on the problem, not finding solutions.

8. Give yourself a break

When someone is rude or cruel to you, take a break from it. Let the situation go, and don't dwell on how badly the person has hurt you. When you focus solely on what happened to upset you, your thoughts are likely to continue looping in that direction forever. Don't expect things to get better if they keep happening; instead, let go of thinking about them and move forward with your life to reach your goal or purpose.

9. Don't make excuses

When you're over-critical of behavior or negatively perceive someone, they can see that you're not concerned about their feelings or well-being. This makes it difficult to move on and be open-minded to the person's point of view.

10. Don't believe your own "facts" and assumptions about someone

When you think you know more than a person about what's going on in their lives, it can be tempting to jump to conclusions and make mistakes about how you think things are for them. This will result in an unnecessary gap between when what is happening and when your assumptions about the person take hold because of your defensiveness.

11. Avoid arguments

When you are defensive, and someone is trying to give you feedback, it can quickly escalate into a fight. When you argue about something, you focus on proving other people wrong. You look for flaws instead of finding solutions.

12. Remember that a compliment is no insult

When people feel unappreciated or taken for granted, they may not see the positive behavior as a compliment, condescension, or criticism. When you criticize someone, you're telling them what they are doing is wrong, harmful, or inadequate when it wasn't. When you understand how someone else sees your words, complimenting them instead can be perceived in a much more positive light.

How to avoid saying things that will make others feel judged or insulted

When someone behaves in a way that bothers or upsets us, we might try to motivate them by talking down to them and making them feel guilty. We might tell them how horrible they are, belittle them or make them feel guilty for something they didn't do.

While these types of comments are sometimes helpful and motivating, they can sometimes make other people feel judged. Also, when you talk down to someone this way, you usually project your feelings and thoughts onto the person. This is different from saying things like "I feel so frustrated because of what you did," rather than telling them exactly what's on your mind about the incident.

When you judge a person's behavior instead of using respectful language or expressing yourself with patience and kindness, you're trying to make them see themselves as inadequate or unworthy of love or respect.

There's nothing wrong with expressing yourself in an angry or upset manner. At times, being aggressive is a natural and necessary response to being hurt by someone. But, there are more productive ways to deal with adversity and situations you find unacceptable.

If you're having trouble being honest with someone in your life, the first thing to do is ask yourself what the benefits will be. When you firmly believe that they should know about their behavior now, you'll be better able to stick to your guns when it would be easier to give up on being upfront about how you feel.

When someone has hurt you or upset you, responding with aggression or anger isn't necessary because it doesn't make others feel hurt or guilty enough. You have to have compassion and say these things calmly and with kindness if they're going to get through.

Wanting what others have

When you feel angry, you may want to make a point of wanting something or someone else's possessions and things. You might want to try to intimidate or even hurt others by making them feel guilty for getting more than you.

Make sure that you recognize when something is your problem, not a person's

When you feel envious of what someone else has, it can be easy to think about how it reflects on you. If someone has something that you want, this might make you feel ashamed, inadequate, or worthless. You might think that all the problems in your life are because of how unworthy and irresponsible you are.

When something isn't going your way in life, it can be hard to accept that there are other explanations for the way things are then blaming yourself or other people. You might think things are only the way they are because of who you are and what you have.

When a person is sad, upset, or discouraged, it can be challenging to accept that what's going on in their life doesn't have to do with them but with how much they're struggling at the moment.

If you're going through a rough time and can't find any reason to feel bad, take a close look at yourself and all the ways you're contributing to getting what you want. Then, look at how you can change the situation to stop making yourself unhappy.

When someone feels unappreciated, lonely, or less-than, they may be working hard to make themselves feel better by creating a list of what's wrong with them and how they're not good enough. They might go through the same thoughts and feelings daily until they finally break down and cry. This reads like a conversation between them, and their self-esteem makes it seem like all the struggles in their lives are because of who they are.

When things aren't going well, it's helpful to write down your feelings about what's happening. It's also beneficial to recognize the other ways you can see your life going well. When you see the good things in your life, you won't feel like "all of this is about me, my flaws, and my problems."

Life is complicated enough without making it harder on yourself by focusing on others' potential shortcomings instead of what's happening in your own life.

Focusing on a bad situation or circumstance instead of seeing it through a positive lens can be hard to keep from feeling like a victim. This makes it easy for people to make jokes about how bad things are and how terrible the world is.

Most people who complain about what's happening in the world don't want to help change things for the better. Most people don't want to see things as unfair, unjust, or unnecessary. They want to point out how bad things are so they can feel better about themselves and so that people can feel bad for them instead of how dependent and helpless they are.

There's nothing wrong with finding joy in how a situation is going or how you're handling it. That doesn't mean that everything is entirely alright or that you shouldn't realize that there are problems in your life. It means that you can appreciate what you have and where you are instead of focusing on how bad your life is compared to others and how much you don't have.

Rather than focusing on your life's insufficient, think about the good things for you instead. Think about how your life could be if you were in control instead of blaming yourself or others for items that aren't going well.

When communicating, it is essential to do so calmly and with kindness. Instead of making yourself feel better or worse because of what someone else is doing or has done, notice how things aren't going well for you. Focus on what needs to change so that they do go well.

You'll likely feel angry or resentful when focused on what people are doing wrong. When you can separate yourself from other people and what they do, you can focus on what your life needs to look like to be positive.

Avoiding saying things that will make others feel judged or insulted is essential to keep in mind. If you think you might say something hurtful or offensive, it's better to say nothing. This can be easier said than done, but when it comes down to it, it's always better to be kind and open than harsh and judgmental.

If you're ever worried that your words will push people away or make them angry with you, then it's best not to say anything at all. People are often more willing to forgive someone who has apologized for saying something disrespectful than someone who has never said sorry.

When people feel uncomfortable around you, they may need to be defensive or put up walls, so they no longer have to feel threatened by you. If you think people aren't being open with you or have turned cold or hostile, you may want to be a little more careful when communicating with them.

When it comes to communicating, you don't need to avoid saying everything on your mind. Sometimes holding onto your thoughts and feelings can make it hard for others to get close to you. Sometimes ignoring what's on your mind is the first step to feeling more centered and peaceful.

If something isn't going well for you, try thinking about other ways that things could be going instead of focusing on how bad things are going for you now. It can help to think about the positive aspects of how you are handling your life right now instead of thinking about how it could be going better.

It can be challenging to want to feel different about your life when you're overwhelmed by all the things going wrong. However, focusing on how things could be better instead of how bad they already are will help you relax and get in touch with what you have.

When someone is feeling negative emotions, it can be hard for them to see a bright side or silver lining to what's going on. You won't see the same opportunities that people who aren't as emotionally invested see because your perspective differs.

When someone isn't in touch with their feelings or doesn't handle them well, they may use humor to avoid getting upset or taking something personally. You'll need to communicate your feelings without taking them too personally or putting them down.

When communication is good and open, it's easier for everyone to understand what's happening. When you're upset or upset about how someone else is communicating with you, it can be easy to go into defense mode and blame them for making you feel bad. However, things aren't always about someone else's intentions or desires.

When other people are trying to communicate with you, don't withhold your feelings, thoughts, or ideas so that you can feel better about yourself. When it comes to communication, it's essential to be honest and upfront so that others know where you're coming from.

As someone going through something difficult in life or who has lost someone they loved very much, it can be easy to feel like everything is hopeless and that things will never get better. Thinking about the good things in your life and how valuable they are instead of dwelling on the negative aspects of life and how futile they always will help lift some of the weight off your shoulders. It will also help you become more content and happy with the life that you do have.

Making it enjoyable to be around will help other people enjoy themselves more and make conversation easier. For some people, thinking about being kind and thoughtful can be difficult. However, when it comes to being patient with other people, it can be easier to ensure that you don't come across as rude or hurtful in your communication.

When someone is upset with you or disrespects your feelings, they may lash out at you or act like they don't care what you have to say or feel. However, if you interpret their behavior as them saying that they don't care, then you won't be able to get close to them.

When you think about what you want from a relationship or someone else and how it can help you feel more connected with them, it can be easier to stay open and have a good relationship. This will also help you keep in touch with your feelings and emotions so that you're in the right headspace to communicate effectively.

Try not to take other people's frustrations or struggles personally when they're frustrated with you or someone else. For some people, it helps them feel better and more peaceful when they get angry or sad rather than worse when they're upset.

When you're in a situation where you are trying to communicate some upbeat feelings to someone who appears hostile or angry, it can be easy to feel confused, uncertain, and frustrated. However, focusing on being calm and patient will help you get through the situation more quickly.

When someone is giving off vibes about how much of a perfectionist they are, it can be hard for them to make small talk with others because they don't want to seem like the wrong person. If people have too many expectations of themselves and feel like everything needs to be perfect always, it can make relationships harder for them.

Conclusion

Communication can be one of the most challenging skills for any individual. In today's highly connected society, those who have a solid foundation of communication skills can be better positioned for success. Be it through verbal or non-verbal language, communication skills are the building blocks for social interactions and professional relationships. There is significant value in effectively communicating with others and reading people like a book. Suppose you don't feel confident in your ability to read others or form meaningful relationships in your professional life. In that case, learning these skills is critical to developing as a leader and achieving career aspirations beyond just climbing the corporate ladder. While all people have unique values and skill sets, highly successful individuals have a few commonalities. If you seek to become a professional with high communication skills, the first step is to realize everyone you encounter has some vulnerability. Through this realization and by developing empathy for others, you can better connect with them on an emotional level. Ultimately, suppose you can establish rapport with someone by showing your interest in them as a person. In that case, you can more effectively communicate your ideas and get outcomes favorable to both parties involved.

It is common to hear people say they are bad at communication or don't know how to talk to people. These people often don't realize that one doesn't have to know something to be good at it. Some of the most brilliant minds in history have proven this to be true. These people demonstrated practical communication skills that are learned and can be improved with practice. Communication is about engaging others meaningfully and understanding the context of what is happening around you. No matter where you are and in front of you, you must develop positive relationships with those around you, your staff team, and department leaders to achieve career success.

Excellent communication skills require a correlation between what we say and what we mean through our body language. Some experts in communication even use gestures when they speak, trying to convey meaning with their hands as much as their voice. Taking the time to observe how others communicate can help you develop your body language and find your language style as well. It is important to note that communication is not always clear and straightforward. It can often be complex and challenging, especially when dealing with people from different cultures or backgrounds. However, building rapport and finding common ground through conversation will be more effortless as you become more aware of how others communicate. An excellent way to start a conversation with someone is by finding commonalities between the two people speaking rather than focusing on the differences that may exist between them. Depending on your goal for the interaction, there are various ways in which you can execute this task.

Since effective communication involves taking into account the context of what is happening around you, it can be used in any environment where practical leadership skills are required. Effective communication is so vital to leading a team that it has significantly improved performance. By developing strong communication skills and becoming more mindful of the context within which you speak, you can better promote the success of your team members and their lives.

While many believe there are no right or wrong ways to communicate, developing your unique style is always a good idea. Pay attention to what people say about you and consider how you want others to perceive your communication style. Consider what kinds of things come naturally to you when speaking with people. Then, choose to focus on those things. By becoming more aware of these issues, you can better communicate effectively and build long-lasting relationships with the people around you.

We have provided an overview of different types of communication and its other components. So that you have a basic understanding of the language used in the professional world so that when you are communicating with your colleagues and other people in any business place, both verbally and non-verbally, they will be able to understand what it is you want to convey.

We have provided an overview of different types of communication and its other components. So that you have a basic understanding of the language used in the professional world so that when you are communicating with your colleagues and other people in any business place, both verbally and non-verbally, they will be able to understand what it is you want to convey.

Communication is essential for any professional or individual. It is vital in building bridges and understanding others. When we communicate with another person, there is a background to ensure effective communication. It is not a one-way communication between two people. It is a two-way interaction. The goal of communication is to understand the other person. It begins with understanding your own emotions. A common trait of successful people is the ability to use their emotions as an asset that helps them better understand why they do what they do and potentially has a positive or negative outcome.

Communication can be further defined as expressing ourselves and our thoughts through words and gestures to get feedback from others, which helps us decide how to move forward in life (personal) or our work setting (professional). It is essential to realize that communication is not just how we express words but also involves understanding the type of communication used by others. This "communication" happens when we observe and understand non-verbal communication.

Here are some ways in which you can improve your communication skills:

Ensure you understand the message you're trying to convey before talking to someone. Be clear about what it is you want to get across to them. This way, the news will come across clearly in the conversation and help the other person understand better what you want from them.

Keep an open mind during a conversation with someone else, be open to new ideas and opinions, and be available for criticism. This way, if the message you are trying to convey to someone is not coming across clearly, then you will be more receptive and engaged in the conversation. Don't take it personally; use constructive criticism as a learning lesson.

Practice non-verbal communication whenever possible. Your non-verbal communication is essential to the message you're trying to convey when talking with others. Please pay attention to your body language, gestures, tone of voice, and facial expressions when communicating so that it comes across clearly what you want to get across in conversation.

Make eye contact when having a conversation with someone. It is a clear sign of interest in what the other person is saying and an excellent way to focus on the exchange. If you're unsure about the message you're trying to convey to another person, find out their views first, then explain yours. This uses active listening skills in your communication and taking notes from the other. This way, you can be more friendly and caring towards others.

Long Distance Real Estate Investing

How to be a Real Estate Investor
And have long term wealth

Christopher Rothchester

Introduction

Long-distance real estate investing can be incredibly rewarding but also carries inherent risks. To help mitigate those risks, you must be informed before investing. A long-distance investor invests in rental properties through a property management company or other professional entity such as a general partner (GP). A GP hires contractors to perform various maintenance tasks on multiple rentals they own and is responsible for finding new tenants when units become vacant.

When you invest in a property near your home, many unexpected costs (and headaches!) accompany the purchase. For example, tenants may request maintenance service after hours, leaving no one available to address their request. Or the general contractor may do a poor job with repairs and leave the property uninhabitable until the work is completed. These problems can be mitigated by completing all renovations before renting and hiring a reliable contractor to manage your properties. However, this approach requires a great deal of time and funding. Consider long-distance real estate investing if you want an investment that can generate additional cash flow but does not require too much direct involvement.

Potential for higher cash flow. A long-distance investor can find more significant properties than a local investor because fewer local investors compete for the same properties. That said, when you visit your rental property, you will want to check on the condition of the units and talk to tenants about how they are being treated. Any negative experiences could lead to fines from the city and a less desirable tenant pool in future years.

A long-distance investor will likely be able to obtain a higher rental yield than a local investor because rent tends to be less expensive when cities are further away from high-demand areas (e.g., cities that are popular with tourists or are known for having a large community of high net worth individuals).

The biggest challenge that long-distance investors face is finding reliable contractors who can complete repairs and renovations in a timely fashion. If you do not have access to a contractor who can complete essential tasks in the same timeframe that they would be completed in your local city, you may want to reconsider your investment.

Frequently, these contractors need to be trusted by the property owner and given access to their funds - funds that are not insured. In the event of an accident, these funds would be at risk. This could lead to further costs and delays if you attempt to complete repairs on a property you do not own or cannot access funds for that reason.

Also, the maintenance cost is often higher for properties over long distances than for similar properties in your city. This is because the contractors that perform these services in your city may already have access to local materials and tools (and maybe more familiar with your local area). While this can still be true in a long-distance market, it can make sense to ask questions about how much it would cost if you were performing these duties yourself.

Different contracts for each property. It is essential to be aware that if you rent properties through a property management company (such as a GP or an LLC), then the terms of your lease may differ from one property to the next. This means you may be required to sign unique contracts depending on what type of tenant you are trying to attract and on how many units you own at a given time. These contracts often come with restrictions and requirements regarding tenants' behavior and responsibilities, making generating income from specific properties easier or much more challenging.

Similar rental properties in different areas. You will want to be aware of competing properties in your area that have recently been rented. Likewise, you may also want to be mindful of properties in your area that have been newly renovated or sold. This can help you determine the overall trend of rental prices before you commit to new investments.

Mixing different property types means finding diversification opportunities with your investment portfolio. If a particular category of property is experiencing a decline, you may be able to invest in another property that is performing well.

Suppose one is looking for an investment strategy for lower initial investment costs and returns. In that case, some long-distance investors suggest going "all-in" by purchasing as many properties as possible in many different locations. It can be easier to find mortgages and loans when purchasing multiple units and hiring good contractors. Property management companies can be more accessible when working with more extensive portfolios.

One of the most common risks long-distance investors face is that their property values may not increase as quickly or quickly as in their local market. For example, while you might be able to buy rental properties that are in high-demand areas and sold at a premium, your initial investment could be higher than it would have been if you had purchased in your local city. This can mean that there is a greater chance of tenants being unable to pay rent on time, that you could own properties with an insufficient amount of assets to cover all of your debts, and that you could face restrictions on how you spend money on the property (e.g., no cash purchases).

There are several essential things to consider when considering a long-distance investment property. This can include your rental market, the population in the surrounding area, basic information regarding your local and long-distance property markets (such as housing shortages or job growth), the type of property you want to purchase (e.g., single-family home or an apartment building), and where you want to buy that property from (i.e., you could purchase from a private seller, from a developer with plans for new construction, or an established real estate firm). Depending on your unique situation and goals, it may make sense to buy locally instead of remotely.

The primary benefit of a long-distance investment is that it provides the flexibility to purchase properties with less cash outlay and higher returns if the properties do well. As you can now see, each property has its own set of challenges in addition to its advantages. But as long as you are comfortable with these challenges and can overcome them, you can ensure a future of passive income as a landlord.

Chapter 1: Is Long-Distance Investing Risky?

Long-distance investing is an investment that requires investing in residential real estate property. Due to the long-term nature of this investment, it is considered high risk, and very few individuals are willing to take on such a deal.

However, it's essential to consider the risks before deciding to engage in long-distance real estate investing. The most common risks that individuals face when investing in long-distance real estate include the following:

a) The investment is subject to fluctuations in the market – like any other type of asset, your property can go up or down in value. Those who invest locally don't have to worry about this since they can keep a close eye on their property and adjust as needed. However, those who support remotely may not be so lucky. While services let you keep an eye on multiple properties remotely, there is no way for you to react immediately should something happen at one of your properties.

b) High maintenance costs are involved – the cost of maintaining and managing your property will be much higher than if you owned one locally. Think about all the time, money, and effort that goes into maintaining a home in your local area versus one halfway across the country. The maintenance costs that you have to pay to include:

Regularly scheduled visits to check up on the property: You may be able to screen tenants remotely, but there's no way for you to personally see the condition of your property or make sure that it's being taken care of. You'll need to hire a professional to check up on the property for you regularly so that you can make adjustments as necessary.

Regular maintenance: Even if your realtor provides a maintenance service, you'll still need to pay extra monthly to ensure your property is appropriately maintained. You may be able to screen tenants remotely, but there's no way for you to personally see the condition of your property or make sure that it's being taken care of. You'll need to hire a professional to check up on the property for you regularly so that you can make adjustments as necessary. You can search for a company that offers pest control services and has a good reputation in your community. This might include bug spray and other highly effective methods to eliminate insects and other pests inside a home or apartment building.

Even if your realtor provides a maintenance service, you'll still need to pay extra monthly to ensure your property is adequately maintained. You can search for a company that offers pest control services and has a good reputation in your community. This might include bug spray and other highly effective methods to eliminate insects and other pests inside a home or apartment building. Hiring contractors: Depending on the type of property you've invested in, certain repairs may have to be done by contractors on rare occasions. However, you'll have to pay for their services if you choose this route.

A professional cleaning service: You won't find a regular maid service in every city and may not even find one in your local area. Depending on the property you've invested in, certain repairs may have to be done by contractors on rare occasions. However, you'll have to pay for their services if you choose this route. That's why choosing a property with many updates and improvements often pay off because it's ready for most renters. However, that doesn't mean there isn't maintenance involved or that your investment will be clean and beautiful when it arrives instead of a complete disaster.

c) There are property-specific risks that you need to consider – regardless of your location, it's essential to be aware of what risks you're taking on with your property. You should avoid investing in a property that doesn't have many people living in the surrounding area. This is especially important if you plan on buying and selling properties quickly because you don't want to end up with an asset nobody wants or needs.

d) There are legal implications – when investing in long-distance real estate, it's essential to understand the local laws and ensure that they allow for this type of investment before purchasing a property. For instance, there are rules regarding the maximum distance you can live from your property. If these laws differ depending on whether you're buying or selling a property, they may not be applicable in your case.

Why do some people not invest long distances?
Investing long distances is a skill that requires hard work, an understanding of the market, and time. Some people don't support long distances because they don't have the expertise and experience to do so. Others fear putting their money into something they cannot see or touch.

To invest long distances, you need a lot of preparation and research into the property, including its location, type, price range, and vacancy rate. It would help if you had schools located in an area with low crime rates to ensure your children will be safe when they go away for school. You need to be able to afford the taxes and utilities. It would be best if you had a reliable lawyer familiar with that state's law. And you need to be connected with a team of people that are invested long distance so they can help you with issues when you get there and take care of any problems that come up while you are there.

Several reasons can prevent some people from investing in long distances; they include:

a) Lack of expertise and knowledge of the market

Market knowledge is essential to understand how and why the market fluctuates. This will allow you to invest long distances with confidence. You will know what to do when a recession hits instead of getting emotional about it and selling at a loss.
You will need to learn about the market if you don't have the expertise. You can join forums like Bigger Pockets and attend real estate investing seminars to learn from those who are successful at supporting long distances or have just started.

b) Lack of capital

Long-distance investing is expensive when compared to a local real estate business. To be successful at this strategy, you have to have enough money saved and ready for investment. After purchasing the long property distance, you can't just sit back and wait for the money to come in. You will have to have a solid plan that covers the expenses of your property.

c) Lack of time

Many tasks need to be completed before you invest in a long-distance property. Although these tasks can be delegated to others, there is always a risk of some things not getting done correctly or on time. If you are busy with work and family, it might not be your best option because investing long distances requires more time than local real estate investing. Long-distance real estate investing is possible with the right resources and tools.

d) Fear of taking on too much financial risk.

Financial risk has to be closely monitored. Some people don't want to take on financial risk at all. If you are one of these people, you need to find a way to overcome that fear or use this strategy in small doses until you are more comfortable with it. It would be best if you had a good plan that covers all the property costs and is executed as soon as you purchase it.

e) Lack of proper education

Information is abundant online on how to properly invest long distance, and it is becoming easier every day to get educated in real estate investing. Many investors are very good with local investing because they have researched long distances before getting involved in this market.

f) Fear of the unknown

Some people fear long distances because they think it is too complicated and not worth it. Fear is a significant obstacle that must be overcome to invest long distances.

What complications would a landlord face if they invest long distance?

Suppose you are a landlord who is investing long distances. In that case, you face many added complications that a local investor does not - for example, maintaining quality tenants is much more challenging. However, there are some ways that landlords can keep their properties in top condition and attract good tenants from afar.

A potential complication of a long-distance investment is that the value of a property will fluctuate over time, which may make it difficult for a landlord to sell and convert their investments into liquid assets.

Additionally, landlords may have difficulty finding tenants when they cannot physically show properties to prospective renters. This means they must find other ways to attract interested parties, including posting multi-media ads on Facebook, using social media marketing strategies like content marketing, and creating attractive profiles on websites like Airbnb.

Landlords may encounter other complications, such as:

a) Inspections

Inspections by state and local governments could prove to be a deterrent to investment. Many landlords have found that state and local inspectors tend to check on the buildings only after people complain about noise or other nuisances. Unless you know a facility is compliant, it may be hard to find tenants willing to accept those risks.

b) Hiring a property manager for multi-unit properties

Hiring a property manager for your properties could increase your investment's value and reduce work since you will no longer have to do all the repairs yourself. However, depending on how many units you own, a property manager might not cover all of them. This means you would need to take care of any issues on your own or hire an additional property manager for your long-distance properties.

c) Financial considerations

If you plan on using financing for your investment, such as with a mortgage, this will present problems if you live in another state or country. Banks are more likely to issue a mortgage if you have sufficient assets in your local currency.

d) Renting out your property

If you plan on renting the property, the landlord must be flexible enough to meet the tenant's schedule. This will require working around holidays and other events that might interrupt travel schedules. Certain items could be difficult for long-distance renters, such as having a refrigerator or stove in place for cooking and an adequate supply of cleaning products and trash bags.

e) Building maintenance

To avoid problems like a leaky roof or other building-related issues, landlords must be willing to hire a property manager and make regular visits to the property. Taking care of these issues will require time and energy, so it is essential to find a reliable contractor.

f) Money management

As a long-distance landlord, you have different time constraints than a local investor. If you invest outside your regular work schedule, it may be challenging to comply with your budget. Assembling new closings could take much longer than in-person with family members or investors.

Some ways can minimize these complications and keep your investment in good condition. Choosing apartment buildings with multiple units can help you manage your time and reduce the problems that a single family may present.

It may be prudent to hire a property maintenance company as they will provide many benefits. A good contractor should be able to provide repairs and maintenance, help tenants with any issues, and also make sure the apartment is clean when new renters move in. Not only will this potentially increase the value of your investment, but it could also lower costs.

What are the risks involved?

Risks associated with long-distance real estate investing are limited, as the investor does not have a physical presence in the property, as would exist with a local real estate investment.

These risks include:

a) The risk of fraud.

As an investment, long-distance investing has a high degree of risk associated with it. Frauds are committed by many types of people, including real estate agents and salespersons, as well as others. In real estate, fraud is known as "swindling" and "robbing."

b) The risk of losing one's money on a wrong investment decision. Investors in commercial properties are at risk when they buy properties that will return less than the purchase cost. With residential properties, investors' ability to recoup the expenses is more limited due to the required time between the time they buy a house and the time they turn it into cash by renting it out or selling it for profit.

c) The risk of not being able to have a say in property management.

Investors cannot have any say in their properties if they decide to let someone else manage the property for them. For example, if the property requires renovations or repairs, the investor may not be able to accomplish this without having a physical presence at their investment location.

d) The risk of increased expenses.

The most significant risk is being unable to manage increased expenses related to the ownership and management of the commercial property.

e) The risk of loss in value due to poor management by another party, such as the manager that has been hired.

Increased costs can lead to a loss in value for the property. If a property declines in value or becomes useless, the investor may have no way to manage or correct the situation, as they have no physical presence at the property.

f) The risk of increased costs from transportation.

The distance can increase operational costs for transportation, especially for commercial properties that require the movement of goods or persons to and from the property.

g) The risk of having a bad tenant.

Tenants can cause property problems, such as damage and nonpayment of rent. There are also risks associated with evicting tenants who do not pay their rent on time. This involves court proceedings that may be costly to obtain compliance with eviction orders, if they are even obtained at all.

h) The risk of declining values in residential properties.

A decline in value can cause an investor to lose money on their investment. This is especially true for residential properties that are not desirable to the general public and have little appeal to prospective tenants.

i) The risk of losses from poor real estate appraisal, such as long-distance property.

An appraisal done from a distance from the property can be inaccurate due to the following:

1. Lack of local knowledge about its surroundings.
2. Incorrect information or "good faith" errors in information input into computer software or other reporting systems used by real estate appraisers.
3. Errors generated by the appraiser themselves due to a variety of factors and mistakes that they may make during the appraisal process.
4. Lack of familiarity with local real estate markets.
5. Inaccurate projections from market research, such as the assumption that an area will grow in value at a particular rate year after year and continue this trend indefinitely.

These risks can be minimized by:

a) Proper research into local real estate markets.

Researching local real estate markets and finding out the projected value of each property will minimize losses due to poor information or assumptions.

b) Obtaining accurate local market data.

Accurate market data on average sale prices and rental rates can be obtained from multiple sources, including local real estate professionals, real estate associations, and third-party market research companies.

c) Using an accurate appraisal process.

Using an appraiser with a sound business practice who has been in the real estate industry for a minimum length of time and has expertise in the property being appraised is essential to obtaining accurate results. Appraisers may have experience and knowledge conducting appraisals in the local markets where they work, which can minimize the risk of errors and inaccuracies in their appraisal reports.

d) Using certified appraisers.

In some areas, real estate appraisers must be certified by a regulatory organization such as the state government before they are allowed to perform appraisals for properties. These professionals are required to carry out their work by the standards of practice set by their certifying body's examiners, which is an added level of protection for investors using this type of appraisal report for their decision-making about purchasing commercial property or other types of investment property as well.

How people do it the wrong way

Most people who are in long-distance investing do it the wrong way. This is because they usually have no experience supporting this way, so they get it wrong. This is because they invest in a property based on the location, which isn't what they should do.

They should invest in "land" or properties that are located strategically and not based on location for the most part. This is because when you invest in an area, you are investing in a type of business, which should be based more on the neighborhood and where that will be.

Then, you can start investing in this type of real estate after you have identified this neighborhood and can see what others are doing to make it better for themselves. This is how rich people invest if they want long-distance real estate investing, but they call it "land."

If a person were to go there and build a new business or invest in real estate, they could make more money than anywhere else. It is the same thing with long-distance investing. While you may have to travel a bit to get there, your investment will pay off more than it would in most places.

This is why most people doing long-distance investing are doing it wrong. They don't know how to look for land or property that will help them make their money back faster than any other type of investment.

To be a long-distance investor, you should start by figuring out where you would like to invest in real estate. Then, go out there and investigate until you find what seems to be the best investment for you. Do not go into this blindly because this is a "business" that can take time and effort. Everyone who wants to make money will have their methods for doing this.

However, here are some good things that everyone who wants to make money from the real estate should follow:

1) Know how much you can afford. It would help if you did not make any investments unless you can afford them in the long run. If you are going to take out a loan, make sure you have all the papers you need to sign before you do it. This is because if

something happens in between and you have to back out, you may have some severe fees to pay for things like the appraisal.

2) Know the area. Before you go out and invest in everything around there, ensure you know everything about your investment and the region. For example, if there is a business around there that can help your business, see if they would be willing to help. If they aren't ready or unable to do it, then try and find someone who can do it.

3) Stick with one part of town. Stick with one piece in the city, and do not invest in everything broadly. If you do this, you will find yourself stuck with a lot of property you cannot sell because it is spread out. Also, there is the risk of stealing your investments from someone who shouldn't have them.

4) Have a price range. If you want to start long-distance investing, you should have a price range for what different real estate investment opportunities are going for. This will let you know if it is worth your time or not.

5) Get a good lawyer. When investing in real estate, you should find a good lawyer to review the papers and ensure they are all right. This is because if they aren't, it can leave you stuck with something you cannot sell or get rid of.

How to mitigate these risks

Mitigating these risks of long-distance real estate investing might be easier than you think. This is not an easy endeavor, and it does require some significant time commitment, but there are measures you can take to reduce these risks. One way to mitigate potential risks of long-distance investing is to ensure that the property you are looking at has amenities your family will enjoy living in, such as a pool or gym. It's also important to only purchase properties with a solid rental history and check their financials before proceeding with a full buyout.

These risks can be mitigated through the following ways:

a) thoroughly reviews the property and the local real estate market. This will help you invest in a property that will generate a positive financial return. It will also help you determine if the property is a good investment.

b) Consider hiring and insuring an agent with expertise on what makes a good real estate investment.

c) Take a careful look at whether or not the property has any potential for appreciation over time. The last thing you want to do is purchase a house with no potential for appreciation and sell it just because there was a sudden demand for this type of housing in your market. Take the time to connect with other real estate investors in your local area.

d) If you want to develop a long-term relationship with a property manager, ensure you find one who specializes in managing long-distance rental properties.

e) Create a network of local contractors, attorneys, and other professionals that can help you keep up with maintenance, improve the returns on your investment, or help you sell or rent out the property if it is not generating enough income.

f) Ensure that you purchase only properties that will not require major renovations and will not require any work beyond one month's worth of repairs when they arrive at their destination.

g) Maintain a healthy skepticism of every deal that you work on. This is especially important when you are working with long-distance real estate investors.

h) Have an exit strategy before making your initial investment. j) Make sure that the property you purchase has an excellent rental history and solid cash flow history before committing any serious money to the property.

i) Make sure you carefully inspect the property and check the rental history before purchasing.

j) Check with local authorities to see if any recent complaints have been lodged against the landlord. If there have been, it's probably best to skip this deal and keep looking.

Tips and tricks

Several tips and tricks have succeeded many top investors in long-distance investing. They include:

a) Developing a long-term plan - Investors need to have a long-term, concise method. Generally, the longer the investing period, the higher the income stream and potential profits.

b) Developing relationships with agents close to the property - Investors need to develop relationships with agents in their home area and those geographically close to where they want to invest.

c) Keeping expenses and taxes as low as possible - Long-distance real estate investing is not cheap; therefore, investors must spend less than expected on taxes and fees, as these costs can quickly eat into any profit you may have made.

d) Finding safe, stable properties - Proactively seeking out secure, stable properties is critical for investors who cannot visit their property as frequently as they may like due to the distance from home.

e) Diversifying - Diversification is critical for long-distance real estate investing, and investors should take the time to research various options before choosing a specific strategy or property. Equity crowdfunding is one option that has been growing in popularity and is an excellent tool for diversification into many different markets and can be a great way to diversify at a lower cost.

f) Finding creative ways to manage the distance - Investors need to find creative ways to manage the space, such as telecommuting, Internet and video conferencing, or using a virtual assistant on sites like Upwork.

g) Dividend reinvestment - Dividend investing is one of the best strategies for long-distance investing and should be considered as an option. This strategy allows investors to have income returns when their properties are not in use by simply reinvesting dividends into bonds or another investment that provides income.

h) Earning less than expenses - Long-distance property investing may require sacrifices to keep costs down.

i) Avoiding debt - Although debt is an excellent way to finance long-distance real estate investment, it can be risky and should not be used unless necessary.

j) Focusing on the long term - Long-distance investing requires an investor to look at the long term and not get caught up in short-term losses.

k) Studying the market - Long-distance investing requires investors to study the market, housing trends, and other factors before choosing a specific property.

l) Finding a local partner or team - It may be a good idea for investors new to long-distance investing to find a local partner or team experienced in this investing.

m) Finding a partner or team with experience in long-distance investing - If investors do not find a local partner, working with an experienced partner is a great way to learn from their experiences building successful real estate portfolios.

Chapter 2: Making an A team

An A team in long-distance investing means that the investor is not only a realtor but also a mortgage broker, property manager, and investment advisor. The A team leader is responsible for generating leads and coordinating the sale or Rental of properties. Because they are involved in multiple aspects of the process, they manage risk better than a typical real estate agent since they have control over what they own while still enjoying some income from renting or selling their properties. The team leader of an A team has to be intelligent enough to pull off this reversal in long-distance investing, which often means that they must be pretty experienced with recent changes happening in the real estate market.

An A team consists of:

a) an asset manager who is responsible for the operation of the team and making sure each member of the sales team is appropriately compensated

b) A salesperson, a realtor or real estate agent who is responsible for selling properties on the team's behalf and takes care of all of the sales processes

c) A mortgage broker who manages mortgage loans and relishes using them as a tool to generate more significant and more profitable deals

d) An investment advisor who handles all financial decisions and studies new ways to improve investment returns. This can be done by analyzing diverse investment options with various companies, including stocks, bonds, precious metals, etc. The advisor may be an individual or a company.

e) A property manager manages the team's properties and takes care of all the associated policies, safety procedures, maintenance, etc.

f) Landlords and tenants who provide the money to buy and maintain the property. The landlord rents out a portion of their property while claiming ownership of all other properties within the team. The tenant can be on a month-to-month basis while paying rent, or they may take up an option to buy and pay rent over a specified period. This is seen in some markets as new development where there are no long-term leases on offered properties, so teams set up monthly lease terms that accommodate investors living in different areas with varying rental needs.

The A team leader has to get a mortgage on a commercial property as soon as possible. It is essential to do thorough due diligence, but if you can find a bank willing to approve a commercial property mortgage even right out of the gate, it will be easier to secure tenants. The commercial property can be used as collateral for obtaining new funding. You should consider the two best funding options: self-certified and private funds. This is where I have found the most success in my real estate investing career.

Once you have a mortgage, you can begin looking for people who need to rent a property. The team leader should be a real estate professional and an investor capable of helping tenants find suitable credit apartments on time. This means they should have access to good databases for placing ads for flats and good references for screening applicants. They should also be familiar with local market conditions to offer advice on what to look out for in terms of scams and help tenants find places that are in their price range. The team leader should also be knowledgeable about all the local regulations, laws, and compliance issues involved in their business.

Finding deals

To be a successful long-distance real estate investor, you have to be able to find deals that are worth taking and, more importantly, can be turned into cash fast enough for you to make a profit.

If you are a motivated individual, you will find deals. Finding deals is a matter of time. It is a lot easier to find bargains if you know what sort of deals you want.

If you are looking for a deal with simple terms, such as two or three-percent returns or something like that, finding deals will be much more difficult. The trick in long-distance investing is always to ensure you get the best recovery for the risk involved.

Finding deals is a lot more complicated than finding good returns. The agreement has to be good for you, and it has to be suitable for your partner. It has to have at least five years of cash flow, and the time that matters is the period during which you will make money. No matter how pretty the return is, if it drops off too quickly, then it won't work. You have to manage expectations accordingly.

When assessing a deal, you have to consider the following:

   a. Cash flow: Does the deal produce enough cash to repay your investments?

b. Opportunity: Is there an opportunity for improvement?
c. Operating expenses: How much will it cost you in terms of time, transportation, and money to operate the deal?
d. Property taxes and insurance: Are you likely to lose money on these over a long period?
e. e) Cap Rate: What is the cap rate on this property by itself, and what is the general cap rate for this deal? If you are buying a multifamily building, it is not a good investment if your cap rate dips below 10%. For example, you are losing money if it falls to 9%.

To be a long-distance investor, you must have consistency in your business dealings. You can't be chasing after every deal that comes along. Once you've found a good deal and made an offer, the process must move quickly and smoothly.

Before you make an offer, you should have your first analysis. This is known as the due diligence process. This process ensures you have all the correct information about the property and the people involved. It's essential in a deal like this. You need to check If the tenant is reliable, and you need to check that there are no liens against the property.

Whether or not a deal will go through depends on how much money it requires, how many people must be involved, and whether or not everything checks out with everyone involved. It also depends on the reputation between the two parties. This is why due diligence is so necessary.

Knowing what kind of return you will get on the property is essential before making an offer. A good deal is a deal that makes money fast and leaves you with a long-term income. A good deal is an investment opportunity that provides enough cash flow to repay the investment, leaving you with some money to put in your pocket and still have a property left over that has potential for growth and development.

When it comes to the offer, ensure you have everything in order beforehand.

There are several types of deals you might consider. You probably will not go for a commercial or construction loan with this property, so you have to be smart about getting the deal done.

Types of deals include:

a. Fix and Flips (single-family homes, duplexes, and apartments that have been abandoned or are not rented)
b. Fix and Holds (you do some work to the place and rent it out while you wait for it to become valuable)
c. Buy and Hold (Long-term investments in single-family homes, apartments, or rentals that need work done before they are profitable. Examples are triplexes, two-family dwellings, condos, townhouses, and commercial office buildings)
d. Pends (are apartments and apartment buildings constructed by a builder or developer and not yet completed.)
e. Rehabs/Renovations (are rehabs of single-family homes or multifamily apartments. These can be renovations of vacant houses, townhouses, or apartments that need work to be done on them.)
f. Short Sales (are properties that are foreclosed or short sales from a bank. These deals can be done yourself if you have the expertise and resources. The quick sale process

can be challenging as you will most likely compete against other investors.)
g. Investments (are investments in real estate that don't require your time, have been renovated or remodeled, and are occupied. These include investment property purchases, commercial investment properties, multifamily buildings, and land for development for commercial purposes.)

You have to make sure that the deal is good for you. What you are looking for is a deal that has the potential for high returns and is suitable for your lifestyle. It would be best if you did not go for the cheapest property because the returns on those properties are low, and the risks are high. The deal needs to be good and will only be good if it meets your criteria. Only a handful of values can provide high returns with low risks, so finding one is essential.

The best deals involve real estate or land in which you have an opportunity to make improvements that bring in more income or allow you to develop the property into something more profitable than what it was before. In other words, the investment is more than just a bank loan.

Estate agents

Estate agents are experts in the real estate market and have access to a wide variety of investment property information. The best estate agents know the local area profoundly and can provide comprehensive advice on what is available. They will be able to advise on which properties are currently undervalued and worth investigating, as well as offer some essential research that can help you decide if it is something that you want to pursue further.

A good estate agent can only provide you with up-to-date and accurate information. They should also have a comprehensive network of contacts, which they can use to get in touch with appropriate landlords who will be willing to rent to you as a foreign investor.

Moving on to another agency might be a good idea if an estate agent cannot provide you with information about at least some properties for sale within your target area. Estate agents who do not understand the market or who do not have access to the correct information are unlikely to be able to help you find a suitable property investment.

However, remember that you can ask more than one estate agent for advice, so if one fails to help, there is no need to give up and walk away.

You can build a good relationship with estate agents in several ways. The first is to go and look at properties with them, but bear in mind that you will likely have to make an appointment. The second option is to approach them with a property rental inquiry. They must be able to list all of their local clients at your visit, so ask if they are willing to take your details and give them a call when the property you are interested in becomes available.

If you are considering moving to one of the properties they manage, it is a good idea to visit the agents and get them talking about the local area. Ask them if they can suggest any schools or other facilities in your target area and if you should be aware of any downsides to living elsewhere.

Finally, it would also be helpful if you could show them a copy of your visa, passport, and work permit. This may help them to understand why you want to live in their area and give them a better sense of who you are.

It is best to keep your expectations realistic when working with an estate agent. Suppose you have provided them with comprehensive information about your requirements, as well as give them any available budget details and personal information. In that case, it will be up to them to try and find a suitable property for you.

Estate agents should be able to help you understand critical issues such as the quality of local amenities and how easy it is for tenants to access local transport links. It will also be helpful if they can outline any issues that might make this type of rental property less suitable for foreign investors. They may also be able to provide support in that they can give you helpful advice about what makes an ideal property for the long-term rental market.

Property management is essential because it can help keep your long-term investment safe and secure. A property manager should be able to help you find suitable tenants, carry out repairs and manage any issues that may arise with the tenants or the property itself.

Coordinating repairs with a property manager is often easier than doing it yourself. They will be able to sort out most problems while ensuring that they do not interfere with tenants' use of your property. They can also ensure that any work is done at a reasonable time and in a way that will not upset tenants too much.

There are a wide variety of property management fees. These usually depend on the number of properties you have, the size of your portfolio, and the services you require. These fees may include the cost of leasing a property to a tenant, paying your mortgage/loan payments, and legal fees. The fees that you will be charged can vary between different property managers.

You will find that many property managers offer a free service to encourage you to use their services and make them more profitable. This could include the provision of free emergency callouts or maintenance services.

However, you must check the details of any property management fees as there may be some charges that are not reflected in the initial price you are quoted or are only included in later stages when things go wrong.

You will need to pay your property manager fees to secure a tenancy; some fees are non-refundable. Before you make any decisions, it is worth researching the different service levels that various property managers offer based on their costs and terms.

Tips and tricks

A power team is critical to any long-distance/remote real estate investing strategy. If you're serious about becoming a successful long-distance investor, you'll need to know how to build this team successfully.

Understanding the best practices of team building and leveraging the power of the Internet by utilizing tools like Skype and Google Hangouts to create a network that can be trusted to help you achieve your goals.

A power team is made up of at least four people who are reliable and trustworthy. These people will be helping you with any investments or marketing efforts required. It would help if you had these people because their job is to get the word out about your company and convince others in your local real estate market that investing in long-term real estate is worth their time.

The following are tips on how to create a good power team:

a) Find trustworthy people.

When you find people who can be trusted, you can build a solid power team. You must discover trustworthy people because your company could get a bad name quickly if you don't. These people will be working on brand building to help you grow your business. Their reputation is also at stake, so you must take the time to interview and vet these people.

b) Find real estate investors who have large networks

You'll need to find someone who knows a lot of real estate investors in your local market. It would help if you found someone who can connect you with local investors so that when you have properties for sale, these people will be willing to buy. This person can work on growing your brand by using their network of contacts to help spread the word about your REI business.

c) Find people who are good at marketing

You will need someone on your team with experience with social media and internet marketing. This person's job is to help find more leads and clients for your company, so they must know what they're doing. If you don't have the money for this position yet, it can be filled by the power team leader if he has the know-how to do it himself or if he knows someone who does.

d) Have a power team leader

A power team leader will be tasked with the duty of telling all of your members what they need to be doing. This person's job is to ensure everyone on the team understands how they can help you grow your business. They will also handle any issues within the group, so you must choose someone who knows how to lead and manage people.

If you want to be financially successful, then you need to manage and lead a powerful team. A good leader not only knows what they're doing, but they also know how to inspire and motivate people. You must influence others with your words and make them see things from your perspective so they'll be encouraged to follow your lead. This will propel you forward in your business and help you reach the financial goals you've set for yourself.

If a team member doesn't have the skills or the know-how to do something, then it's your job as the leader to teach them or find someone who can fill in the gap. You might be able to do some things on your own, but it's better to have a team of people who can help you achieve your goals and make your business successful.

It's essential to find people with a good attitude because you'll need to be able to depend on them. Their ability to follow through on things will depend on their perspective. If they have a bad attitude, you'll always have problems with them and constantly feel like you're babysitting someone. It's better for everyone that someone who can work hard and do what needs to be done without having an attitude about it is chosen for your team.

Investors

Investors are looking for investments where they can earn a return on their money. An investor buys assets such as stocks, bonds, and property to make a profit. The key is to buy low and sell high; that's how investors make money.

There are two basic types of investors: speculative investors and long-term investors. A hypothetical investor buys assets that they think will appreciate in the future. The hope is that the gains will be more than the losses incurred by holding for a longer term. The opposite is valid for a long-term investor who buys assets with low risk and minimal chance of losing money in a short time.

There are several ways through which you can find an investor. They include:

a) Family and friends

Family and friends are one of the best sources for investors, and this is because they already know you and your business plan. They can offer helpful advice on whether you have a realistic chance of succeeding. Since they trust you, they will be more likely to invest in your business. Family members and friends can also act as mentors to help your business grow.

b) Angel investors

An angel investor is an affluent individual who provides capital for a business start-up in exchange for a percentage ownership in the company or simply an ownership interest without taking part in the management. Angel investors are usually successful businessmen or women with extensive experience managing their businesses.

c) Venture Capitalists

A venture capitalist is an investor that invests in high-growth companies which are not yet profitable. They tend to favor businesses and industries they know well and can understand easily.

d) Crowdfunding platforms

Crowdfunding platforms enable entrepreneurs to raise funds online from many people, typically via the Internet. Some sites are general, where anyone can post their idea or project, while others cater to specific groups of investors, such as charitable donations or alternative energy projects. Platforms charge a fee and offer a commission based on the money invested through their website.

When talking to an investor, you need to tell them the following things:

    a. how much money do you need? This will allow you to ask them how much money they are willing to invest in your business.

    b. why do you need their money? It would help if you gave them a logical explanation of why you are seeking financial help from them.

    c. what will they get out of it? Investors want to know whether they will get any benefits by investing in your company or not. They want to know if they will eventually see profits; after all, it is said and done.

    d. how much money do you need to get through the initial stages of your business? It would help if you told them how much money you will use to buy equipment and raw materials and hire staff. You should also include estimates for marketing and other expenses that may arise in the future.

e. explain what risks they will be taking by investing in your company. It would help if you told them the risks involved in investing in your company, such as losing their investment or even not making a profit.

f. explain why you are qualified to run this kind of company and be successful. It would help if you told them what makes you eligible to invest in this business. If your business plan includes a franchise, you need to explain why that particular franchise is a good choice for them.

g. answer any questions they may have about your company and its background.

Investors will want to invest in your business if your plan is sound and you have a record of success. It would be best if you showed them that this would be profitable for them and you. They may search for other investors interested in your kind of business if you meet with no success after getting bids.

Lenders

A lender provides you with capital in the form of a loan or line of credit so that you can use it for future projects. Generally speaking, lenders are willing to lend money to people with a history of being able to pay them back and will give you more favorable terms than banks.

There are several types of lenders, including hard money, private money, and private lenders.

a) Hard Money Lenders

If you're looking for funding fast and with little hassle, hard money lending is the way. You won't have to fill out application forms or jump through any hoops, but your interest rate and repayment terms will be much more expensive than a bank or a traditional lender. Keep in mind that if you can't repay your hard money loan on time or miss a payment, the interest rate on the loan will soar at the lender's discretion.

b) Private Money Lenders

Unlike hard money lenders that typically lend out small amounts, private lenders loan out more significant sums of money. They are generally more willing to work directly with real estate investors. They are looking for a much better return on investment than what they'll get from the bank, but they understand the risk involved in long-term real estate projects. Getting personal lending terms is relatively easy, but you may have to jump through some hoops. There's a lot of paperwork involved when securing a loan with a private lender, including agreements, LOIs, and other official papers. You'll also have to provide collateral or equity for your loan or line of credit.

c) Private Lenders

In most cases, private lenders are a kind of hybrid between hard money and private money lenders. Usually, these lenders offer lower interest rates than conventional loans and work directly with real estate investors instead of using intermediaries like private money lenders. In most cases, these loans provide less leverage than a bank.

Finding downline members may be the best route for you if you're a real estate investor who wants to build an extensive network of investors. With the power of social media, creating a robust network is easier than ever. To use this strategy, you must ensure that your network is active and working hard to make money. You must maintain relationships with your downline members and monitor their progress to ensure they're also making money.

Finding lenders for your project can be challenging, as only limited numbers are available in the market. However, you should seek out your network — friends and family members — who might be interested in lending money to someone they know. You could also approach potential investors at networking events or meet people through social media channels.

Finding a suitable lender is just as important as finding a good partner. If you are looking for a short-term loan, for example, your lender should be able to let you have money quickly. If the lender does not have funds access, it is better to find someone else.

The most important thing is to find a lender that will give you favorable terms and conditions. Before agreeing on any deal for a loan or line of credit, make sure that you have done your research thoroughly, so it is best to gather information about them so you would know what kind of people they are and why they should be in business with them.

Accountants

Accountants are a vital part of any business, including real estate investing. If you consider going into long-distance real estate investing, you will need a good accountant to track your finances. If you hire an accountant, they will be able to help you with all your bookkeeping needs. They will also be able to help you with paying your capital gains tax on time, which the federal government requires.

To find an accountant, ask a real estate investor involved in long-distance investing for the name of their accountant and see if that person can recommend a good one for you. Another way you can find one is by calling nearby accounting firms and asking them if they know an excellent long-distance real-estate investor that uses their services.

After choosing a company to use, you will also want to select an accountant from that firm. If you choose an accountant directly from the firm, they will often charge you more because of the convenience of having an account with the firm. If you do not mind, choosing an accountant at a different branch in town is a good idea. This way, you can save some money in your account.

If your accountant is a real estate investor, they can tell you if they think it is wise for you to invest long-distance or not. They also have knowledge of which types of investments are better than others and what time frame will work best for your investment plans. Your investment plans can then be decided upon from this knowledge before any real money is spent on the project.

You will want a good accountant to ensure you pay the appropriate tax on your real estate investments. If you plan to be in this business long-term, you will also want to know what investment will work best for you. With the help of your accountant, this can all be done before any money is invested in a property or project.

Tax returns are made every year, and some laws can cause you to have to pay back taxes on the income that you have received. The good news is that the federal government allows all those who own real-estate investments to be a little irresponsible with their taxes and still be able to invest in a real-estate project without paying back any income tax for being unresponsible.

If you are considering investing long-distance, you will want an accountant who knows how to keep all your investment accounts straight. This will also help them know if any of your accounts will require more work than others or if it is even necessary for you to hire an accountant at all.

Accountants can help you keep all the money you make in your investments, but be prepared for them to want to help out with other accounts. How accountants help with business accounts can vary from accountant to accountant, and finding one that will work best for your business is essential. If they have experience working with real estate investors like yourself, they will also be able to tell you if they think that long-distance real estate investing is going to be a good idea or not.

You can find a good accountant by asking other long-distance investors for recommendations, or you can also look at any accounting firms in the area and call them to ask if they know of any good long-distance investing accountants nearby.

Find a good accountant willing to help you with your business accounts; there are a couple of ways you can do it. You can ask a long-distance investor for the name of their accountant, or you can request an accounting firm in the area if they know of any accountants specializing in long-distance investing. If you choose an accountant from the firm directly, they will often charge more because they get paid based on how many clients they have.

Even though accountants are vital to any business, you should not expect them to give you hand-holding services. They will manage your accounts for as long as you need them to and then let you run your own business when it comes time for the annual tax returns.

Contractors

These are simply individuals who are paid for their services and obtaining clients. They will either be professional contractors or manual laborers. Manual laborers are self-employed, and the only form of income they receive is from their labor. Professionals do not always have to be business owners, but most contractors in the construction industry must own a business. Ownership usually consists of building a company or having someone make it for them with their hard work, savings, and contracts with customers

Builders are essentially contractors who build real estate. They don't have to work for anyone and can offer their services to many clients. They, too, receive their income from customers, but the cash flow is usually a more robust option, unlike contractors.

There are different types of builders, they include:

a) On-site construction contractors

Customers hire on-site construction contractors to build their property. The contractor works on-site, helping the customer with the building process. They have all the paperwork in order and can guarantee quick turnaround times. Customers don't have to worry about anything except ensuring the contractor is on time, able to work, and provide top-of-the-line services.

b) General Contractors

general contractors hire other builders and do not construct their buildings. General contractors get paid a higher hourly rate than site-built construction specialists because they usually perform all of the labor themselves, including managing subcontractors and overseeing activities at every stage of a construction project.

c) Design-Build Construction Contractors (DBCC)

These are builders with enough education and industry experience to take on all aspects of a project. Design-build construction contractors begin designing and building a structure before being given the final building plans. They usually work with architects, owners, and engineers from the beginning of the design process, allowing them to create better designs and save customers money.

d) Specialty Builders

Specialty builders focus on one particular aspect of construction, such as remodeling, restoration, or conservation. They must undergo training to become licensed master builders to run a business in their area of expertise.

e) Custom Builders

Builders who construct a home from the ground up. They will design the house according to their client's wishes and build the home on a tract of land they own or lease.

Most builders can make a living if they provide quality service and have good references. They should have basic building knowledge, communicate well with customers, be trustworthy and manage costs wisely while keeping customers' needs in mind.

There are ways in which you can use to find a builder; they usually include:

a) People-Focused marketing strategies

This is where you use the Internet to contact potential customers. You can throw free events or meet-ups and attract leads that would like your services.

b) Personal recommendations

This is where you ask and listen to what other people say about the builder's services, costs, and quality. Contact references will be willing to provide you with excellent feedback about their experiences with a particular contractor/builder.

c) Referrals

It is always better to get a referral from someone you trust because they can give an honest opinion about how well someone ticks every box for good customer service practices and how reliable they are when it comes to being at work on time, and how efficiently they work.

d) Cold calling

Cold calling is a strategy to contact businesses and offer them your services. You do not need to have any prior relationship with the company; all you need to know is its name and number. An excellent cold-calling strategy is creating the correct script, ensuring you are well-prepared, and always having a follow-up plan.

e) Trade associations

Suppose you are a new builder or contractor. In that case, it is wise to join trade associations because they will be able to provide you with multiple benefits, including valuable information on how to run your new business efficiently as well as guidance on what industry standards are legal and acceptable. They will also be able to put you in touch with other professionals who may become customers or contacts in the future.

f) Working with branding agencies

Research has shown that it is better to use a professional branding agency to help you with all aspects of branding your new business. They can even handle social media marketing and lead generation and help spread the word about your business through various mediums.

Negotiating with a builder can be challenging because they have many different clients, and you compete for their attention. They should have excellent communication skills and positive, upbeat personalities. They must be able to start on the right foot to build a solid relationship with their customer.

They should be willing to listen carefully to customers' wants and needs, provide them with excellent customer service and work within their budget so that everyone can end up happy with the results of their contract.

The negotiation process will differ from job to job and from customer to customer. A contractor must be flexible and willing to meet their client halfway on specific issues like cost. They should always keep the relationship professional and polite, even if a customer is angry or upset about something. A good builder can handle the situation calmly, professionally, and diplomatically.

Chapter 3: Using the Internet to Find Deals

As you may or may not be aware, finding a long-distance real estate investment property just got easier with the advent of technology. It's not that unusual these days for people to use the Internet to find deals. So why is it becoming so popular? The answer is quite simple; because it works! With sites like Zillow and Trulia, you can search listings from thousands of homes across the country, comparing them against local prices in your area. This will allow you to find opportunities at a wide variety of locations and buy a home for less than what it would cost if purchased locally.

The Internet has expanded to a nearly level playing field, forcing market forces to ensure local pricing is competitive with the national average. Thus, if you're interested in finding an investment at a price that doesn't consider your paycheck, it's time to try it. It only takes three quick steps.

a) Find an investment opportunity you'd like to purchase and research the area. This is the most challenging part of the process, and it can feel like a daunting task if you don't know what you're looking for. It would help if you got educated on current market trends, local rules, and property values. It's important to know if any restrictions prevent or discourage your purchase (zoning, deed restrictions, etc.). This step requires a little more effort than the others, as you have to do some research online.

b) Determine how much your potential investment costs before researching the market price of similar properties in your area. I like to work with one of our agents who has access to more information than anyone else on this site would be able to uncover. They call this "Stealth Mode," which does precisely what the name implies. Once we establish a market price, our agents will find the number of comparable listings in your area at that price. This makes it much easier to determine an approximate purchase price you can afford.

c) Once you accurately estimate this investment's value, begin the search. You've done all the hard work; now take a deep breath and ask yourself if this investment is something you'd be willing to put your money behind. If so, it's time to find a buyer for your potential investment property!

There are several advantages of putting together an Internet-based resource. A real estate investor can be accessed online from almost any location. You can use websites like Zillow (and many more) to search for properties and value them based on local pricing. Many of our clients use this approach to identify an area where they want to invest; then, our team will do extensive research, looking for a property that would be a good fit for their investment portfolio.

Different types of property sites to find deals

A property site is designed to help people find, purchase and sell properties. Property websites are like auction sites; they usually list all real estate items instead of just one type. It might be a house or an apartment building. Usually, someone could live in or rent out this type of property. In the past, investors might have spent hours or even days driving to find lots of possible places that they could purchase. Today, many new real estate websites allow people to search for properties online and look at data about the property and its neighborhood.

There are different types of property sites, they include;

a) MLS (Multiple Listing Service) Sites

These sites have a database of all the real estate currently for sale in a given area. It's organized by city, with each listing having a picture of the home or property, details like the price, and the name of the realtor who represents the seller.

b) For Sale By Owner Sites

This is where you can find properties for sale by someone who is not a professional realtor. This means they usually sell their home for less than they would if they hired someone to sell it. Many of these sites will allow you to search by location and even price range, which helps inspire better deals.

c) Vow of Silence

This is where you can find out about properties not currently listed on the MLS. These tend to be properties that only have a few days on the market, and they're located in areas that aren't high-traffic. This means they won't get as many potential buyers looking at them, but if you're looking for something more specific, this might be an excellent place to start your search.

d) Foreclosure Sites

Banks use foreclosures as a way of getting rid of homes that they can't sell. They usually sell them for much less than the current market value. These sites can help you find homes starting at a lower price point, sometimes as little as a few thousand dollars.

e) Land Banking

Investors use these sites focused on buying properties with the hope of redeveloping them to grab higher property prices in the future. These sites focus on smaller plots of land where investors plan to create their new development in a neighborhood. The investor might build an apartment building or housing development and sell off the individual units once they're complete.

f) Commercial Real Estate Websites

These are the types of sites you would use if you're looking for commercial real estate. These sites focus on more commercial-focused properties. Commercial real estate is usually a property that will be used for business purposes, like retail space, factories, and large office buildings.

g) Short Sale Listings

Short sales are homes that the owners can't sell with a traditional listing, usually because of financial difficulties or because they need help to pay off some debt. Short sales are much cheaper than other real estate types, so these sites list them in hopes that someone might be interested in buying one of them at a discount price.

Tax records

Investors can be able to acquire deals through tax records. When the new operator pays, a property changes hands and the tax amount. This amount is then transferred to the new owner's tax account, which can then be invested in private equity, hedge funds, or other real estate investment funds. For this to happen, the old owner must provide a copy of their tax forms for this transaction.

The long-term wealth you will accrue from this process includes a lower personal tax rate due to low capital gains taxes and additional investments already in progress (such as private equity). Buying properties through tax records is only one form of long-distance investing that can offer tremendous amounts of return potential based on your investment strategy and goals. With the right approach, you will be able to acquire the necessary funds for your real estate investing and achieve a greater degree of success.

Having total control over what will happen with your money is something else that makes long-distance investing an excellent option. So many variables can occur within short periods, driving long-distance investing a superior alternative to traditional real estate investing. It's important to continuously build upon your existing knowledge base because it will make all the difference when capitalizing on your investment opportunities. You can create this base in various ways, including online courses, workshops, seminars, and conferences.

Forfeiture property is a property that is seized by law enforcement or other agencies because it is involved in some illegal activity. Forfeiture property includes money, vehicles, and property that is considered contraband. All forfeited properties are subjected to sale at public or private auction.

In most cases, seized properties are offered for public auction before being sold privately. If the property does not receive any bids during the first two weeks of a public auction sale, then the property will be sold privately to another party. Properties that have received multiple requests during a public auction will receive an additional five days before being sold privately to the highest bidder.

There are strict conditions that must be met to participate in a forfeiture sale. The seller must have title to their forfeited property, they must have possession of the property, they cannot be prohibited from selling their property, and the value of their property must be determined.

The standard property forfeiture process is broken down into various steps. The first step is titled 'Seizure.' Police or other law enforcement officers serve a notice in a public place that details all the information on the forfeiture. After receiving a response, the officers will search for contraband or illegal activities within their jurisdiction and then make an arrest. This arrest ensured no criminal activity occurred when law enforcement served the seizure notice.

The second step is titled 'Forfeiture.' This happens when a judge confirms that the property can be forfeited or sold. If the judge determines that the property can be seized, it can proceed to have its title transferred through a court order. The property owner can file an appeal if they feel they were not involved in any illegal activities and think law enforcement officers wrongly seized their property.

The third step is titled 'Disposition.' This occurs when no appeals are made, and the property has received its title transfer through a court order. The next step would be to advertise the public auction sale or find a private buyer for your forfeiture property. If the forfeiture property does not receive any bids, the property will then be sold to another party through a private sale.

The fourth step is titled 'Sale.' This occurs when the title of your forfeiture property is transferred to someone else. If real estate investing is done correctly and using proper legal processes, there are many potential benefits from investing in forfeiture properties, including low-interest rates, bargain pricing of property, and quick closings.

The fifth and final step is titled 'Expiration.' This happens when you have paid off your loan and have no further obligations under the agreement. Forfeiture properties have a seven-year expiration date. If you decide to sell your property, a buyer must be willing to purchase your property within seven years. If the sale does not occur within this time frame, the parcel will be re-forfeited to law enforcement to keep it out of public hands.

Social media

Given the opportunity to invest in a property, investors are often too scared to take that first step. There is always the fear of picking the wrong location or being too short a time for such a significant investment. Fortunately, there are platforms like Facebook Marketplace and Craigslist that help allow investors to break into this market without breaking their budget.

An excellent way for new investors to start is by utilizing social media websites to purchase properties from less experienced or resourceful sellers who may need help selling their homes before they can relocate or settle in with family members. This social media approach works exceptionally well in the country and city where you have a local support network.

Social media platforms such as Facebook Marketplace are an excellent way for new investors to break into real estate investing by purchasing a property that needs to be sold quickly. Through social media, a real estate investor can reach an investor looking to sell their plush house in Florida or the family home in which they live in Arizona. Through a classified site like Facebook Marketplace, you can connect and make an offer on that property.

Social media can be an attractive way to locate potential real estate investments and investors who need a quick sale of their property. To get the most out of social media, investors must utilize their networks, and networks must also use social media for advertising their products.

Instagram is another great social media site to connect with potential sellers and buyers of real estate. In addition to regular social media like Facebook and Twitter, Instagram is a great way to market your product or provide information about your business. If you want to build a following to get more exposure as an investor in real estate, Instagram is the platform to utilize.

When you post on social media, you must include details about yourself, including your location. Still, it is also crucial to connect with people with a similar interest in real estate investing. By following the right audience on social media and posting helpful content on their page, investors can build their brand by creating connections with others they otherwise would not have made or found if they were not active on social media.

Individuals can get properties through these platforms by suggesting to the real estate seller that they can market their property. By exploring these social media platforms, an investor can gauge how much interest and how many views he will get from his listings. Only properties that have received multiple views with high-interest levels will be purchased in some instances.

The advantages and disadvantages of using these social media platforms are;

Advantages

a. Social media allows for prestige for land and real estate investments in a relatively short period.
b. Investors can buy real estate without using cash through bank loans or mortgages.
c. Social media makes it easy to negotiate with sellers looking to sell their properties quickly and at a low price so that they can access funds they need for other major purchases or family needs in other locations.
d. The use of social media allows investors to create an audience on which they can market their investments and business ventures which could lead to a greater return in the long run.
e. Social media allows investors to see the response they receive from online customers and write good reports and reactions on social media.
f. The use of social media allows investors to connect and interact with each other through likes or comments to mingle with people similar in interest and discover new sources of real estate investments.
g. Social media makes it easier for investors to build their brand to get more exposure when it comes time to market their products or services.

Disadvantages

a. The use of social media can lead to individuals making false claims about property prices, locations, potential tax codes, etc., which can lead to future problems for the landowner.
b. The use of social media is not always efficient. False claims about real estate investments on popular sites such as Facebook and Instagram make it very difficult for investors to purchase property at a reasonable price quickly through marketplaces like these because potential

sellers become scared off by false information that they are receiving from other customers or potential customers who have used this same platform.
c. Social media is not always a quick way to gain exposure for your real estate investments, and often the success of social media on these platforms relies on what is referred to as "clout" or "popular pages."
d. The use of social media and other marketing methods are not always reliable ways to get real estate sales. There have been times when investors have paid thousands of dollars in fees through social media marketing when the actual costs can be significantly lower.

Due diligence

The key to becoming a successful real estate investor is always doing your due diligence. The research you put into a property before purchasing it will go a long way in helping you avoid financial mistakes and make intelligent decisions.

The principal first step to doing your due diligence on a property is continually researching the neighborhood. Being informed about the area you want to invest in is essential for identifying which properties are a good fit for you. You can use crime statistics, school information, assessors' data, and hot neighborhoods as a starting point in your research.

Once you know what areas might fit your needs and establish that there will be no problem closing on the property, take the time to do it right by inspecting with an inspector before putting in any offers on a property. The time spent checking and discussing items with the agent will help you better understand what makes this property tick and allow you to negotiate better terms.

A checklist is a great way to keep track of things when looking for property. You can make a checklist of items you want to find out about the property, like how long a house has been in the neighborhood, how many units it has, and if it is a bank-owned property. This will help you determine if this investment would fit you well. Use a checklist to keep track of your wants and needs while looking at properties.

When buying a property, check the following:

Is there sufficient parking? What utilities are included in the rent? How much of a deposit is required? Do you know who will be your tenants? If not, how can you find out more information about them? Are any issues with the property now affecting tenants or the buyer? What can you do about those issues, if any? Is this an income property or one for resale? Does it have room for improvements or additions to increase its value over time, like adding a finished basement, attic or additional units on site to help it bring in more revenue over time?

When it comes to buying a property, some things are red flags. If you find out a court case with the property or if it was sold many times in a short period, you should consider taking your money elsewhere.

If there is no parking or the boiler broke at the same time you want to make an offer on the house and will be needed for winter, think twice. If there are properties that have broken down pretty recently but are still for sale, this might be a warning sign of problems with the neighborhood or management company.

When researching homes, check "red flag" areas such as crime statistics and foreclosures. Is the neighborhood or street a good area for your investment, and is there something you can do to help raise property values?

Here are some tips and tricks to consider when purchasing a property,

a. Have a reputable and experienced real estate agent in your corner that you trust for buying and selling properties. You will have to make many decisions quickly when purchasing real estate, so you must have someone with experience to answer any questions you may have. A real estate agent can also help negotiate a great deal for you on properties before putting in an offer.

b. When deciding to purchase a property, make sure there is enough return on your investment before putting down an offer. If the homeowner is asking for more than the house's value, consider offering less instead of overpaying for the property and losing money immediately.

c. If you are investing in a mortgage-free property and the lender is asking for more than 1% down on the property, you will have to decide if this is a good deal for you. If the property has been operating as an investment and is not working at a loss, it may be worth paying extra.

d. When buying a home or investing in investment properties, ensure that your agent has inspected the property before making an offer. If there are no issues with the property, surprises can happen after the inspection before you close on it.

e. Always research the neighborhood and surrounding area before looking at a property, such as crime statistics, school information, assessors' data, and any hot communities, to see what is going on. You can also use online resources like Zillow.com to get this information.

f. Always have a checklist when looking at properties and stick to it while looking at them. The more you know about the property, the less time you will spend on the look, and more time can be focused on the negotiation of going forward.

g. Always use a real estate agent when buying properties. They can help your feel comfortable in purchasing a property, negotiate and understand if you are getting a great deal; things like title and acreage issues can be dealt with by finding out before they get to the point where they might cost more than just paying out of pocket as opposed to trying to find out afterward with an attorney or even worse, having to foreclose and get rid of a home.

h. When buying real estate and negotiating a price, don't be too hasty in making your decision. Take your time and think about it as often as you need before settling on a price. You can also consider talking with an attorney or, even better, an agent specializing in real estate law if there are any red flags regarding the property or neighborhood that might affect your buying decision.

Rental checks

A rental check is a check that is sent to your bank account each month as you collect rent from your tenants. These checks make it easy for the landlord or tenant to track finances and record payments online. Familiar with landlords, individuals can also use this check.

A favorite of real estate investors and landowners, a rental check makes it easy for people to get paid on time from their tenants without relying on a personal meeting up with their tenants every day. The tenant can also make payments via the internet if they prefer this.

Rental checks are straightforward to set up with your bank account. This can then be used either as a landlord or even for individuals that want to collect rent from their tenants. Your rental check consists of several documents from your landlord to your bank account every month. These documents vary by bank but sometimes consist of an authorization form, lease agreement, and payment notice. The lease agreement will most likely be in the form of an electronic lease agreement (LEA) that can be signed online by both the landlord and tenant with their respective computers, making it possible for both parties to sign the lease electronically. The landlord then uploads the electronic lease to their bank through their landlord's website.

Next, your rental check will be delivered to your bank account. These checks consist of an invoice, receipt, and payment record if you are online and make internet payments. The amount will change depending on the current interest rates and economy in that region of the country. Someone from the bank usually does this, or it can also be done electronically, which makes it easier for payments to go directly into your account or for expenses that cannot go directly into your account to have a paper trail of evidence if needed later.

There are many ways that you go about checking prices on rooms and single lets. The first would be searching online for the area you want to visit, such as a hotel or a space rented out daily or weekly. Once you have identified these rooms, the next step is to make an appointment with them to view the room and check whether they have a rental agreement. This is also very time-consuming, but it is worth it if you are looking to rent out an entire house or apartment unit on your property.

If this is not possible, you could call the landlord or make an appointment with them in person or by phone. It is also essential to check your tax records and documents, which will have the information on what you paid to rent out a property back in the previous year.

Some rental checks are very accurate and have a high level of precision, while others can be slightly off. If you have ever owned a rental property, then you probably know what I am talking about, as it is always hard to calculate payments and come to an agreement on the fine details that can sometimes differ by a few dollars.

To avoid this problem, you should follow these tips:

a) make sure that you check out the bank and make sure it is a good one. You want to ensure the bank is reliable before making any deal with them for your real estate investing needs and acquiring rental checks for your properties.

b) make sure that the bank is a good one. You may have heard of some banks that are not so good, and you want to stay away from them. You do not want to deal with the hassle of getting scammed by these banks. If there are any issues with these banks, they will most likely not give you a great deal on your real estate investments, no matter what you have in place or what kind of deals you make.

c) make sure that it is a real account. Many people use multiple accounts for their savings when they first buy their first property as this can be useful for many things, such as tax records and paying utility bills. These accounts are outstanding, especially if you are a new investor looking to invest in a rental property on your first try.

d) check out what kind of forms need to be filled out. You can get a rental check without having to fill out many forms, but some banks do require some information that needs to be filled out for you to get the best rates and fees on your account.

Each bank will have a different set of forms that you need to fill out for them to get information about you and your property. This will depend on what bank and type of account you are trying to get.

e) search for personal preferences regarding what kind of document the bank has their customers fill out. Some may ask you where you will be living and other more personal questions, while others won't ask you as much.

f) make sure all the information is correct. Some banks offer online accounts that are not updated often and can be hard to follow. It is straightforward for mistakes to happen with your accounts when it comes down to filling out these forms, especially if they are not readily available online.

Here is an example of how the rent would typically be calculated:

"Real estate investors use rental checks" for several reasons. These checks make it easy to collect money from your tenants, as well as from the landlord, at regular intervals. If tenants do not pay their rent, they can get a "default notice" that gives them thirty days to deliver. A landlord can also issue a default notice. After 30 days, the landlord has the right to deduct the payment amount from their account held in escrow. If tenants do not pay after 60 days, they may be subject to garnishment, taking money directly out of their bank account without notice.

When you view the rent amount on a rental check, you may see an invoice date that indicates the day the landlord sent it to you or a notation to indicate "Last Acceptance," which means the last date of acceptance. You may also notice rent adjustments for months when no rent was paid. The landlord does not need their tenants' permission to charge for late rental charges, which can be quite costly in some states, such as California and Florida.

Rental checks are used by real estate investors, who have property management responsibilities, to collect money from tenants. They can also use them to collect from landlords.

Digital viewing

The rise of the internet has seen a surge in the popularity of long-distance real estate investing. Investor websites, blogs, social media communities, and conference calls have made it easier for investors to get acquainted with new homes. However, this digital trend is fueling the rapid rise of what's been coined as "the Web 2.0" – or being a real estate investor on the web rather than in person.

Long-distance real estate investing works best when done partly online while working with a few on-site visits over time to check out properties. The internet allows for a much more efficient process. Still, it doesn't make a long-distance investor any less vulnerable to scams or fraudulent agents who may take advantage of the fact that people are too far away to see their actions.

However, by thoroughly researching your market, you can feel confident in your decisions and do this online. Long-distance investing not only allows you to avoid certain risks that come from buying a property through a broker or agent, but it's also an effective way of mitigating scammers' and fraudsters' attempts on your money.

Google Maps is a tool that long-distance investors widely use. This can be advantageous because it has information to help you make an informed decision, but it can also be a significant source of frustration. It would help if you learned the tips on using Google maps effectively and what features are available to you.

You can also find a great deal of information about local restaurants, shops, and other businesses through online searches. This will allow you to get a feel for the area where your property is located and whether or not it would be convenient for you or your tenant.

While it's an excellent tool for learning about a neighborhood, face-to-face interaction is the only way to assess your area accurately. You can't see the quality of a local school, how busy the streets are, or what kind of relationship you might have with your neighbors online. Google maps can give you an idea – but only one–about properties available for your investment and areas in which you want to invest.

It's also important to note that long-distance real estate investing can be affected by things that aren't always visible on Google Maps – such as water damage in buildings and the presence or lack of sidewalks in certain areas.

One of the most effective strategies for a long-distance investor is to go through a walkthrough performed by an estate agent. This allows an investor to get a better sense of the home and neighborhood in person while also getting some questions answered by someone with local knowledge.

Some investors can make more informed decisions during this process, while others may find that it confirms their earlier perceptions. Whatever your experience is with walkthroughs, you should consider doing one before embarking on your investment to try and avoid surprises with the property once you've bought it.

There are several advantages to doing a walkthrough in person rather than just looking at photos online. For example, a walkthrough will immediately put you in touch with local real estate agents or brokers who can answer any questions about the property.

You may be able to have a look at a few different properties and decide which one is the best fit for you; since it's on-site and not through an online search, you won't find yourself disappointed with the house or neighborhood that's shown to you.

Knowing your neighbors is one of the best ways to ensure that your investment will be profitable. You can also make connections and get a good feel for the community where you're investing – and this will save you a lot of time trying to figure out an unfamiliar area on your own. Finally, walkthroughs are an excellent way to meet the neighbors.

Although, some investors dislike going through a walkthrough because they feel self-conscious and vulnerable. Most people who do this are new investors and don't have the experience to react well to negative feedback. This can make it challenging to choose a property you feel comfortable with, especially if you're not used to the real estate industry and don't have a trusted broker working with you.

Apps to help you

An application is software that corresponds to a specific task. Some apps, like PayPal, Google Maps, Yelp, and many others, are helpful for day-to-day life; others focus on particular activities such as photography or shopping. And there is one type of app called real estate apps, which help you achieve your long-distance real estate investing strategy.

Different apps that help people invest in properties include:

a) Facebook

Facebook offers a new service to private advertisers who want to sell their real estate to the platform's users.

b) Zillow Instant Offers

Zillow Instant allows homeowners to post their properties on the site and get in touch directly with prospective buyers. Sellers set the price and payment terms – so if they want cash, they can specify that.

c) Realty Mogul

This app allows people to invest in property in markets as close as their hometowns or as far away as Silicon Valley without ever leaving home! Realty Mogul helps match investors with property listings all around the United States so everyone can take advantage of this booming industry.

d) Instant Offers

Buyers can use Instant Offers to create a shortlist of homes they want to see in person. This app allows homeowners to list their property on various social media platforms, including Facebook and Instagram. When the list is ready, the app will send out requests for showings and arrange itineraries so that people can easily visit the houses they're interested in purchasing.

e) Webuyanyhouse.com

This app connects local sellers and investors interested in buying homes at no cost and selling them after the renovations have been completed, making it easy for everyone involved to get what they want out of the deal.

f) OpenDoor

OpenDoor is a peer-to-peer marketplace that connects sellers directly with buyers. For example, in San Francisco and Phoenix, Open Door lets buyers browse through a library of listings from homeowners who are anxious to sell – without paying any commission fees.

g) Depop

This app lets people buy and sell clothing and other fashion accessories locally. Users can arrange in-person meetups or mail their items to the buyer once they make a sale.

h) OfferUp

This app allows people to buy and sell locally. The app includes a chat function that will enable users to ask sellers questions and make offers before they're ready to meet up with them.

i) Wallapop

Wallapop is a mobile marketplace for buying and selling secondhand goods. With this app, people can browse through the Wallapop database of items for sale, locate the ones they want in their neighborhoods, and arrange a time to meet up with the seller.

j) TradeGecko

This app helps companies determine which marketplaces they should use to sell their products based on real-time data about which platforms are generating the most demand.

Chapter 4: Keep Up to Date With the Market

Keeping up to date with the market is key to developing good real estate investing skills. It's also essential to sell when the time is correct, which requires a solid understanding of how best to avoid paying too much or not enough. Many excellent websites are available for investors to use for market research and up-to-date market information so you can constantly adapt your approach as you invest.

A long-distance real estate investor benefits by accessing these resources from anywhere in the world during business hours. The long-distance investor avoids the need to take time off of work or other commitments to travel as needed. Investing through those resources keeps them competitive with a local investment group focusing on their local time zone rather than international markets where they would have more competition.

Real estate investing is an excellent way for long-distance investors to gain real estate investments, but it's not the only way. When you have an effective business plan and a desire to expand your wealth and add to your bottom line, any new opportunity that looks solid and offers good returns can be considered. You can broaden this by venturing into new business lines, such as wholesale, retail, or online buying and selling goods or services.

Keeping up with your local real estate market will help to keep you competitive. You don't have to pass up on potential opportunities just because you live out of state from where the option is located. But it would help if you were careful that you don't get so distracted by the latest investment that you neglect your business. Become familiar with local laws, regulations, and customs, as most areas of the country operate differently. This is an excellent example of how a long-distance real estate investor can stay competitive in a challenging market while taking advantage of nationwide and international opportunities.

Property prices

Property prices are at an all-time high. This is an excellent time to invest in real estate, but you must be mindful of the risks to take advantage of it.

If one wants to track property prices, here are some steps one opts to follow:

a. Track the price of properties at all times: This is the essential requirement to check the trend and ensure that property prices go up or down. If a person wants to track property prices daily, they need to monitor the market. Property professionals provide access to today's data and ensure everything is going well in their area of interest. If one has dated real estate market research information, one can see how real estate prices have been compared with others depending on their chosen time.

b. Keep tabs on past trends: Property price trends are an easy way of knowing whether or not investment opportunities exist in certain areas within their locality. Tracking property price trends gives you a good idea of whether there is a probable chance that prices of properties have gone down in certain areas. This is an excellent investment time, but you must check on your area's current real estate agents to ensure everything goes well.

c. Check on local real estate investment opportunities: Keep tabs on the latest investment options available at this point and understand their pros and cons for better results throughout.

d. Take advantage of property prices when they are lower than usual: Property prices dropping below their average market value is an excellent reason to invest in real estate. Property investors take this opportunity and invest in properties they want at this point. They can make this decision because they understand that there are chances of property prices dropping and not rising by the end of the year.

A property can be valued by;

a. First in - first out method: First in - first off (FIFO) is the simplest method of valuation that most investors use. This method is applied to property values too. In this way, the cost paid for the property is considered its current value compared to other properties of similar type and location. One should check on the FIFO method to get a better idea of property valuation by using some of their properties as examples.

b. Comparable sales approach: Although this approach is subjective, it is considered one of the most effective methods most investors use. This way, a property's value is determined by the cost of other similar properties. They can also use a market analysis to establish these values.

c. Third-party valuation: This method is used by those who are experienced in real estate investment and know the right time to invest in property. In this cheap method, a third party finds the property's value by comparing it with other similar properties, including current price trends within their region. If one is interested in getting property prices from this source, one needs to contact real estate professionals so that everything can go well for them in the future.

d. Cost approach: This is the least precise method to determine a property's value. In this way, one needs to know the replacement cost of a property they want to make their investment successful. All they need to do is check on some of the real estate agents in their area and know how much it would cost them to build a new house or buy another existing one.

e. Market value approach: This method requires data from similar transactions. One can also use anecdotal information from other sources (i.e., tax assessment and sale comparison). The market value approach can be used by investors who want to invest in less-liquid properties to increase their investment returns over time.

In terms of real estate valuation, some factors should be considered;

a. "Market value": One of the key factors determining a property's overall value is its market value. Real estate investors should consider this in their analyses because it includes the current market prices, sales trends, and historical trends within their city.

b. "Multiple": A multiple is calculated by dividing a property's cost by its current value. If one looks at property values, one will see that, in most cases, it is between 1X and 10X, depending on the locality where they are investing. In some cases, it can even go up to 20X or 30X. Using multiple increases the chances of getting more returns over time.

c. "Growth potential": A property's value is a good indication of its growth potential. Many real estate investing companies use this particular technique to determine if they want to invest in a specific property or not. This is the area that investors will want to focus on, getting an idea of how much a property can grow in the future.

d. "Price/income": A property's market value has been calculated by considering income from its annual rental income. When this is done, it will tell investors whether a particular parcel is reasonably priced or not at any point in time. If a property's market value is too low, it can lead to less money made in the future. In many cases, one will see that if a property's market value is lower, it can be tough to make money in the end.

e. "Book value" is another essential factor in real estate valuation. In this way, investors will ask their real estate agents for an estimate of when the values of properties may go up or down by using this method. This will become essential, especially when buying secondhand properties, because most property buyers are required by law to use this method for buying such property.

f. "Player/operating costs": In many cases, property values are affected by the operating costs of a particular property. These costs will include mortgage payments, taxes, and insurance. If a property's market value is too high, this could reduce the profit margin for investors. This is based on the idea that if a property's market value is higher than its operating costs, it might not be a good time to invest in real estate.

g. "Costs of sale": A property's value will directly affect the closing costs required for selling it over time. It will also affect the amount of liquidation needed to sell it out when the time comes to do so.

Should you buy when property prices rise?

When property prices rise, there are many reasons why it's tempting to buy property if you can afford it. When prices rise, you may think you will be able to sell the property in a few years for more than you paid.

However, if buying a property is a long-term investment, it's essential to consider whether buying now will help or hinder your chances of achieving this goal. If the market becomes less favorable in 3-5 years and property prices have fallen by between 15%-30%, selling your property for less than what you paid for it will result in a loss.

So, should you buy when property prices are on the rise?

Yes – as long as buying this particular type of real estate makes sense based on your situation. If you're planning to stay in the property long-term, the benefits of investing in property are huge.

For example, the gains on some types of property can be huge, and you may even be able to achieve your investment goals quickly.

If you buy when property prices are rising, it will be harder for you to sell in the future. It could also make your initial investment feel much more significant compared to what you have left; however, if you're thinking about making a short-term investment to raise money for something else (such as having kids or buying a car), don't buy.

If this is the type of property you're considering investing in, consider looking at how long-term real estate investing will benefit your situation. (ie. If you plan to buy a home and stay in it for at least five years, then buying won't be the best choice. However, if you're looking to sell after 3-5 years and use the money from selling to build up your savings account or pay off debt, then investing in property is a great option.)

The advantage of buying property when prices rise is that you can raise the equity in your property very quickly. The more property equity has, the lower your mortgage will be on that house. As such, if you're trying to get rid of a high loan-to-value ratio (LVR), then buying at the current market price will likely make it easier for you to do this.

If you're always looking to sell your property at a profit, then buying at the market will make it very likely to achieve this. However, if this isn't what you want to do, you must consider how long-term investing in property can help your situation.

Should you buy when property prices crash?

When property prices crash, they fall substantially below the average selling price. In other words, property prices are low. Property prices are low because there has been a lot of new housing construction over the last few years, and people want to move into these new buildings. This has pushed up demand for houses, meaning that even if sellers are not asking anything near the home's original price, it is still challenging to find buyers without reducing their price significantly.

You may have heard of the saying, "cash is king." This is what all real estate investors strive to amass, whether they are flipping houses or purchasing rental properties. Cash, as you know, allows you the freedom to buy and sell the property. Cash means you don't have to rely on other people or institutions for financing or operating capital. Cash means you can purchase property at meager prices and sell it at a profit. Cash means that if something goes wrong, you can walk away from the deal with some money in your pocket rather than worrying about the lender taking your property from you. It is important not to confuse cash with liquid funds. You can use liquid funds for an acceptable period without having to wait for a check or wire transfer for them to clear

1. Cash, however, is different because even though it may remove very quickly, it doesn't mean there has been any real change in your financial position. You still have the same resources as before you purchased or sold the property. Cash is just a number. No matter how large or small, it means little to no change in your financial situation. This is why it is essential to consider what value you are getting from your cash. If you view yourself as a cash investor rather than a property investor
2. then investing in property may hold little appeal for you. It s something that you do once the desire for more money has gone away. On the other hand, real estate investors want a return on their investment and are willing to put in extra effort to do so
3. If that's the case, investing in rental properties can help you achieve this goal
4. Rental properties will allow you to get the cash you need while also gaining a rental property that can yield a positive cash flow every month

5. You make an income-producing and liquid investment when you add these two things. If you are still wondering what cash flow means, it is the amount of money (after expenses) left over after your mortgage payment from rent checks.

If one buys when the property prices crash, then the income from rent and any other money left over from selling a property will be sufficient to pay your monthly bills. However, as mentioned above, this is not something that most investors would be interested in doing. That is because one of the purposes of investing in rental properties is to generate income. Even with real estate prices down, these properties pay more than enough to cover the mortgage payment while giving you more cash flow than if you were renting.

How to get below-market-value deals

Getting below-market-value deals means buying properties at market value and then selling them for a profit. This requires you to find deals in places where supply exceeds demand. These are usually cheap areas that are not the best places to live but produce good income through mortgages or rent.

Getting below-market-value deals also means identifying the right places in which to find these below-market deals. You can find them by focusing on factors contributing to high demand and low prices. These include:

The first important is where you are most likely to find properties in your area, such as large cities. Next is the price range of what you are willing to pay for a particular property. Also significant is the number of available properties at each price point, the level of competition, and how much time it takes to find a great deal and put it on the market.

Farmland and other undeveloped properties can be purchased at low prices. The trick is to find out of the land can later be developed and then price it according to how much it would cost to create it. If you are unsure, consider taking guidance from real estate agents or experts in the industry.

If you want to get below-market value deals for a single-family home, you should go for a foreclosure or a bank-owned property. You can find these homes easily through a quick search online. More significant properties such as ranches, farms, and commercial buildings may require more research to locate the right price point and level of development.

Overall, there are loads of ways to get below-market value deals. It requires you to do your research and be patient. You can also take the help of real estate agents to help with transaction costs once you have found a promising property.

Rental rates increase

To be clear, there are many reasons you may want to invest in real estate, but one of the most important is that rental rates are more likely to increase without fail. When rental rates rise, it's an easy decision to start looking into investing in real estate. When rental rates increase, it can give young investors a head start on older investors, and you'll be able to make money for just about as long as the market lasts.

It's important to note here that rental rates only go up. For example, if you fixed a property at $1000 rent per month, it would be rent-controlled until January 1st of the following year and last for one year. If you select that property today at $1200 per month, your landlord can increase all their rent to $1200 without needing approval from the city. That's an important point because it gives you a significant head start on older investors; to make money on an investment like this, they need to wait for a minimum of about four years before buying their next rental property.

A common misconception with rental properties is that you can buy a property and then wait for the tenant to pay for it for you; many people like to make excuses about why that doesn't work - "the property market is down" or "the tenants are bad" are everyday things I hear. But there's no point in making excuses if you're not fixing the problem. It's also important to note that in some markets, tenants may not be as good as you think they are, the market could be terrible (think 2008-2009), and you could lose money. So even with good tenants, these properties require a lot of work because of their risks.

Increased rental rates are an excellent time to buy, but if you're looking at it from a long-term perspective, buying a vacant property is the best way to go. When the vacancy rate increases, so do the market rate. And as we've seen before, when rental rates go up, landlords are more likely to sell or fix their properties at higher prices because demand is so high and supply is low.

Chapter 5: Structuring Your Deal

Structuring your deal is a fundamental part of real estate investing. Structuring your deal correctly can make you not only live off property income but also generate wealth. The most important aspect of property structuring is that the asset is split into different pieces so that no person can use it to gain net wealth directly. An unscrupulous or inexperienced investor may convert the rental property into their own and live off that income. This will not lead to long-term wealth but will cause you to work much harder than if you owned the property via traditional means.

There are two main ways to split your investment. The first is to break it into multiple people. This can be done via a partnership, but it is much more challenging to do and get right. The second is usually done through a limited liability company or an LLC. An LLC will act as the property owner rather than any person in the company owning said property. By structuring your deal correctly via an LLC or similar entity, no person has any more significant share of your investment than anyone else on paper.

The most crucial reason for structuring your deal correctly is that someone can not make themselves rich by taking money from your rental property by committing illegal acts regarding your investment. This book will explain two ways in which you can be cheated. The first is through an unlawful act on the part of a third party which you discover, and the second is when someone within your company commits a crime that would make them liable to be sued.

Structuring your real estate deal involves dividing up your asset so that you have multiple entities, each with its owners. The most important aspect of this is ensuring that no person has any more significant share of ownership than anyone else –a rogue investor cannot directly profit from the property for their gain. Lastly, we will cover how to avoid liability when someone within your company commits a crime.

An LLC is the most effective way of structuring your rental property. An LLC can be created by filing paperwork with your local government and getting an EIN from the IRS. An EIN is a unique tax identification number that will allow you to file taxes for your LLC.

The most accessible type of LLC to create is called a single-member LLC. This means that there will only be one owner of your company, which will own the rental property. The downside to this method is that you have unlimited liability for any problems with the property or money in it – if someone gets hurt, you are held liable. You can be sued directly due to ownership of said rental property.

The second most straightforward and standard method of structuring your real estate deal is via a Limited Liability Company. An LLC is much more complex than a single-member LLC and has many more benefits, but it can be mighty in the right hands.

It would help if you understood that all cash flow streams need a structure for you to reach success as a real estate investor. This can be done via low-interest rates, no-interest rates, or other methods such as investing with leverage or carrying debt. Let us help you find a structure that works for your deal and budgeting needs.

Legal structuring

Legal structuring means structuring your real estate investing company to build a long-term business while minimizing tax liability. One of the most common legal structuring methods is using a limited liability company or LLC.

If you are new to investing in real estate, it may seem like a daunting task to start learning about this process. However, when you understand how it works, investing in real estate becomes more accessible and more profitable than ever before.

The easiest and most common way to invest in real estate is through a limited liability company or LLC. This is the simplest way to get started with legal structuring.

If you buy property as an individual rather than in the name of your LLC, you will be taxed on the profits when you sell the property. The tax rate for an individual can be as high as 50 percent for federal and state combined and up to another 4 percent for local taxes.

However, buying through the company will protect your assets from lawsuits and make a profit when you sell your investment properties at a higher price than what you paid.

Your company will also be taxed, and you will receive a W-2 which shows the profit you made from your properties. If you do not distribute these profits at least annually, you can have your LLC taxed at the highest rate of 35 percent.

The advantage of buying through an LLC is that you do not need to report the profits to your Social Security account or pay taxes. You can also receive a K-1 on form 1065, which shows a Schedule

K-1 where the profit you made from your investment property is stated and how much money went to whom. You can then keep track of any excess profits and distributions.

Furthermore, if you do not have a problem paying the taxes on your cash flow at a later time, you can also delay your capital gains taxes until you decide to sell your investment property. This is important as it allows you to avoid paying capital gains tax year unless you choose to take the money out. A common strategy is making money through rental properties and using it for passive income by buying real estate loans yearly [or until sold].

Some people even use their real estate LLCs for other business ideas, such as starting a website or creating an online business. In this case, you could use the profits from your company to invest in another business idea.

When you decide to buy personally, you should be aware that the IRS treats LLCs like a partnership and the tax laws are pretty different from an individual. For example, losses incurred by an LLC are limited to their income and cannot be spread around to other members.

However, an LLC has more flexibility than an individual and can make things easier on your taxes. For example, if one of the members of the LLC has a substantial amount of debt, they can use it to pay taxable interest-free money to the other members as a passive investment which is not taxable.

Another advantage is that you can split up the properties and ownership among other family members. This makes it easier to use gifted money to purchase real estate, especially if some family members do not want their names put in public records when buying or selling your properties.

However, having several owners for one piece of property will complicate things if you wish to sell that property at some point. You need to be aware of this when you buy a property for investment purposes through an LLC.

In most cases, LLCs are more complicated, and we advise you to use an attorney to help you decide which option is the best for your situation. They can also help guide you through starting and operating your LLC.

You should remember that if you choose to operate as an individual, there is no up-front cost. Still, when it's time to sell or buy properties, it can be tricky to pay capital gains taxes on all profits yearly or even to determine which profits are taxable and at what rate they are taxed.

Property management

Property management is a broad term that generally refers to the process of managing real estate property. It can be handled by local property management companies or controlled by the property owner. In either case, property management entails overseeing buildings and their day-to-day operations. This includes the management of tenant relations, rent collection, repairs, and any other issues that may arise.

Knowledge about the local real estate market and experience managing properties is essential to succeed in property management. You should also maintain strong business relationships with lenders and work with an attorney on lease agreements. Networking within your community is also essential because you will likely manage properties belonging to people you know.

Another reason real estate professionals like property managers are so effective is that they know the market trends and local real estate conditions. They know when a market is on the rise or falling and can negotiate with tenants to get a better deal. This allows them to get more money from each tenant, boost their profits and give them higher values for their properties.

The easiest way to manage your property is to outsource it. Many real estate management companies handle your properties' day-to-day operations. Property management companies typically charge a flat fee based on the annual gross income of your parcels. In some cases, they may charge a percentage of rent collected or a price on collection of rent.

Suppose you use a property management company and do research and comparison shopping before hiring one. It is essential to work with an ethical and reputable company that will improve your profits and provide honest management services in return for their fees.

When looking at property management companies, ask them to provide samples of their work. This way, you'll be able to see their work style, if the work is done correctly, and their costs. You should also know if they will provide you with benchmarks of how much profit you can expect from their services.
Relationship-based property management companies are a good option for real estate investors because they are more likely to give them access to individual properties and keep them informed about everything that is going on in the building. They may also be able to save you money because they have

relationships with vendors who can help reduce costs throughout the year. However, they may be more expensive than other companies.

If you want to manage your property and save some money, there's nothing wrong with doing so. However, unless you're wealthy or want to spend time working on your properties, it's probably best to outsource this task to a local property management company you can trust.

Tenants

A tenant is an individual or company that rents property from a landlord. The tenant pays rent to the landlord in exchange for the right to use and occupy the leased premises, typically for a fixed period.

A tenant has physical control over real estate but usually does not own it outright. The rental agreement is one of several contracts between a landowner and renter, determining how much each party will contribute toward expenses such as taxes or insurance. A contractual agreement is subject to laws regulating such agreements that vary widely throughout countries and regions.

There are several types of tenants, they include:

a. Residential tenant, a person who lives in the demised premises and is responsible for paying rent to the landlord.

b. Commercial tenant, a company that pays rent to a building or a building section as their office or shop. Due to the increased number of disputes between landlords and tenants over possession orders and other issues, this type of tenant has recently received much attention from the legal system in many countries, including Singapore, England, and Australia.

c. Business Tenant, corporate body rents rented premises to carry on any business or trade. Due to the increased number of disputes between landlords and tenants over possession orders and other issues, this type of tenant has recently received much attention from the legal system in many countries, including Singapore, England, and Australia.

d. Governmental Tenant, which is a public authority (such as a department or board) that occupies property leased by the public administration rather than a private person (such as a company or organization).

e. Pensioner Tenant. This type of tenant is usually defined as one who receives rent from an aged person to live on their behalf.

Reference checks verify a person's rental, employment, and credit history. Typically, the tenant must sign a document declaring the truth of their stated information. This is an essential tool for landlords who are recovering from a bad tenant and want to avoid future tenants having similar issues. The tenant is giving their word that their stated information is accurate. This document is known as the "deed of warranty."

Though some tenants may have legitimate reasons for not paying rent (e.g., job loss), they may be more likely to lie. If the tenant appears unstable or has a pattern of late payments, tenants may be more inclined to cheat. They may spend more than they should perform services not required by law (such as installing air-conditioners) or break other rules with little concern for the consequences.

Landlords are also responsible for property damage and injuries from tenants and guests. For example, if a faulty lock on the door injures a tenant, the landlord will most likely be held responsible. A landlord can also be held accountable for physical damages caused by employees' negligence (e.g., a maintenance worker allowed water to leak from a building's air conditioning system into one or more apartments).

Both landlords and real estate agents do credit checks to determine the ability of a prospective tenant to pay in full and on time. They are essential for long-term leases or tenants with no prior rental history. Credit checks may also be required for some city/municipal housing authorities, for which a credit check may be required before approval.

There are two standard credit checks: direct checks (obtaining information from lenders) and non-direct checks (obtaining information from sources such as the credit bureau). Credit checks may be considered intrusive if they reveal damaging details that are either irrelevant to the proposed tenancy (e.g., a bankruptcy that occurred during a tenure with another landlord several years ago) or could be used for forgery (e.g., a tenant's name has been changed to a fictitious identity).

Credit checks are necessary because they allow landlords to evaluate prospective tenants' financial responsibility and value. They help determine whether a prospective tenant may be capable of paying all the rent, whether payments can be made on time, what their financial obligations may be after vacating the property, and whether they are likely to cause damage to the property (e.g., by failing to pay legitimate utility bills). However, landlords should recognize that high credit scores do not mean there will be no problems with tenancy due to an inability to pay rent or other issues.

A good tenant can positively impact a building, while having a bad tenant living there can hurt other tenants. They may not pay rent, they could cause damage to the property or neglect it (by failing to make necessary repairs), or they might create problems in terms of noise nuisance, harassment, or other forms of antisocial behavior. In addition, some tenants may take out loans against their properties and become unable to repay them if interest rates rise.

Some applicants may be more suitable for one tenancy agreement depending on their income, financial obligations, and other factors. For this reason, landlords must use caution when screening applicants for a residential tenancy. They should be aware of the type of tenancy agreement (e.g., fixed-term or periodic) to ensure they make the right choice.

Landlords need to take into account factors such as the local environment (e.g., pollution), proximity to public transport and recreational facilities, proximity to workplace, etc., and whether these are attractive enough for tenants who may be willing to bear much higher costs of living in exchange for a better quality of life or better convenience. Landlords should also consider the tenancy's value to ensure that both parties are satisfied with the terms. Some tenants may be less inclined to pay rent if they believe it will be cheaper elsewhere.

Process of buying a property

Buying property is a long-term investment, both in time and money. There are many things to consider, such as location, the property's condition, financing, and the amount of work you expect to do on the property to make it sellable. If you are going to invest in real estate, then that's great, but if your goal is just a quick profit, which is typical for investors who don't care about investing in real estate, then there are plenty of other ways for them to achieve that goal within their industry.

The process of buying property involves the following steps:

a) Viewing the property

This is where you confirm the investment by checking out the location and ensuring it's suitable for your plans. During this process, ensure you don't get emotionally attached to the property and keep an open mind about where you will find a property to buy. I have seen investors get emotionally attached to a property just because they like it, this is a mistake, and you should never do it.

b) Researching the properties

Once you have decided on your property, you start researching as much information as possible about the history of the house, who used to live there, if any violent crimes happened in or around the place, and so on. These things will be important in negotiations later on. It would help if you also tried to find the neighborhood as much as possible. The information you gather will help you plan your renovation and ensure that your investment will succeed in the long run.

c) Contacting the property owner

Once you have all this information, contacting the property owner is where it all starts. Most properties are owned by a company that acts as a landlord and not directly by the property owner. If this is the case, you need to contact that company and ask permission to buy. Suppose it's an individual, then making them an offer will be more complicated but still possible. If you have never purchased property before, it's best to use companies that have been doing it for a while, as they will have the experience to help you along the way.

c) Deciding on a price

Having contacted the owner and found out how much they want for their property, you should decide whether your price is fair enough for your plans.

d) Financing

Financing is one of the essential parts of the real estate investing process. Many different types of real estate financing are available, such as private money, home equity, hard money, etc. The best funding for you will depend on your goals as an investor; if your goal is to buy houses cheaply and fix them up, then getting private money might be best. But if you buy the property and rent it out, getting a loan from a bank might be your best option. Finding a lender who will lend you is vital if you don't have the money to pay for your property.

d) Performing inspections

Once you have paid for your property, then the work begins. Although you won't be able to do much at this point, an inspection can give you an insight into what state the house is in. It's best not to make repairs at this stage because doing it now will increase your costs and make it harder for you to get good resale value later.

e) Renovating the property

Renovating a home involves making the place habitable, so it's marketable and sellable to buyers. When you renovate a property, you should ensure it is as safe as possible, especially after purchasing a house that has been in crime. For the house to sell quickly, many improvements should be made. The most common enhancements are to the kitchen and bathroom, but there are many different options available, and you can find some on my website.

f) Selling the property

After all, the work has been completed on your property; then it's time to sell it and make some profit. At this stage, you should ensure that everything is in your favor as much as possible and make as much profit as possible. If you are buying a property to rent, make sure it's marketable so that tenants are interested in it; this way, you can charge higher rent and make more money from your investment. If you plan to fix the property but keep it for yourself, making sure the house suits your needs is very important. You don't want to buy a home with no space and no storage, for example, when all you wanted was a prominent place with lots of storage.

e) Renting the property

Choose the right tenant carefully if you plan to rent a property out. Putting up an ad on a website is an excellent way to attract people but choosing them based on their experience and personal life is more important. No matter how good their references are, make sure you do your check before signing anything or giving them the keys, as that's when you will have to be most careful. You might have just paid a lot of money for your property, so it's best not to make mistakes like this.

Chapter 6: Managing Property in Different Cities

Many people who live in big cities or have an eye on retirement try to diversify their investments. While they should invest in properties closer to where they live most of the time, long-distance real estate investing is another option.

You can get more value from your investment by managing properties in different cities. This is because:

a. You have a wider choice regarding where to invest your money.
b. You can invest in properties in another city that has already proven itself over the years. Some cities are booming, others have been experiencing problems, and others have been unable to keep up with the competition.
c. You access the markets of different states and countries through primary or secondary cities.
d. The rental yields on some of these properties are higher than those on similar properties in your home market. In addition, you will receive an international income stream by operating these properties as owners rather than managers.

However, the benefits of long-distance investing are real and permanent. These properties can be sold after ten years, and the capital gains of the original investment will not be small. In addition, you do not need to be an expert on markets or the real estate business. But things get better when you are a long-distance real estate investor who is also an expert on markets and real estate management.

While in different cities, you can visit these properties more often than your local investments. This way, you can catch the problems before they get out of control. If a problem is critical, you must have it fixed immediately. If this is not possible, you must find qualified tenants who will pay the rent on time and manage your property more professionally.

The best way to manage your long-distance property is to do it yourself following these time-proven principles:

a. Visit regularly and get involved with what's going on with properties, tenants, and the management company. There are no excuses for not taking care of your business.
b. If a problem takes place, solve it immediately or find a solution that will prevent it from getting worse.
c. If you cannot solve a problem or find a solution, then see the management company's point of view. It is always good to know that your opinion is not what matters.
d. On every visit, inspect every property and note all problems.
e. Keep track of how much time you spend managing these properties and consider reducing your workload.
f. Be sure to manage your tenants in a friendly manner. It is advisable to communicate with them through phone calls or emails to keep your relationship intact even when you are not in the same city.

Having a system and process in place to make it easy to manage
Having a system and process in place to make it easy to manage your property, and not necessarily the conventional way of having standalone sales offices and traveling a lot. A long-distance real estate investor may maintain just one property but diversify

their investments to have enough capital for many properties at once.

The long-distance real estate investor system has well-lubricated and easy-to-manage properties, you don't have as many properties as an office-based investor, but you have the potential for a lot more. You can have a property for every time zone, country, or continent because you aren't tied to having any office.

Having a system and process to make it easy to manage your property is not necessarily the conventional way of having standalone sales offices and traveling a lot. A long-distance real estate investor may maintain just one property but diversify their investments to have enough capital for many properties at once.

A real estate investor system can consist of leaseholders, self-managed teams, partners, or affiliates. A long-distance real estate investor can also be in the same country or region as the properties they manage.

Long-distance real estate investing is not about hard work and sweating out in a rental unit all day. It's about having a system and process in place to make it easy to manage your property, and not necessarily the conventional way of having standalone sales offices and traveling a lot.

Long-distance real estate investing is where the idea of being self-manager fits in very well. You have the freedom and flexibility to choose your hours, which allows you to live the lifestyle you want. But with that freedom comes responsibility. You should not do this if you are sitting alone in a house and not making any money. It's something you should do if you are going to be involved at some level, whether you're the one that collects the rent or if you have some management company managing your properties.

One of the main advantages of long-distance real estate investing is that you can find very motivated sellers. This can help you get a good deal, or at least one better than the local investors would get. You will not have the same face-to-face contact with your tenants as an owner-occupant would, but you also won't have to worry about getting repairs done on time and dealing with unruly tenants when they move out.

Keypads where tenants can keep keys

A keypad can be installed on the exterior door or a tenant entry door to provide the tenants with access to their unit, but it can also be installed in a stairwell. Each tenant has a code they enter to gain access, and if they forget their code, there is usually an override feature that will allow them to reset it or have it emailed or texted to them.

The ultimate goal when installing a keypad on a stairwell is for tenants who live upstairs from one another not to have the same code for entrance. This will help secure both units and make the tenants feel more at ease about having visitors stay over.

Each tenant must be given their code or code permission to allow visitors access. If an individual tries to enter their neighbor's apartment or even the stairwell without a key or working code, it will alert the landlord and management team. This way, if there are any issues with a tenant who may be letting strangers into their unit, it can quickly be investigated right away. Be sure to let each tenant know which door they are assigned and any other codes they may need to give out in an emergency. Most buildings require all tenants to have a key to prevent potential break-ins.

This is also helpful because if two or more tenants live on the same floor, they will often communicate. If a tenant is out for an extended period, their neighbor may have been asked to check on their apartment and ensure it is secure. Since neighbors are often either friends or family members, having them access through a keypad entry makes things much simpler for everyone involved. It also prevents having to change the locks every time a tenant leaves or enters the unit and will save you money in the long run.

There are also other gadgets and equipment that the landlord can use; they include:

a) motion detectors

These are extremely useful in many situations. Their primary use is to feel safe that no one will be breaking into your unit, but they can also ward off unwanted visitors (pets, children, etc.).

b) Glass break sensors

These are used for the same purpose as motion detectors. The only difference is that they are inside the unit. They will sound an alarm if any glass breaks within the unit or from a neighboring unit(s).

c) Bars on windows and doors

These bars are used to prevent people from entering the building without authorization. They are installed on windows and doors to limit how much someone can enter or exit your unit. They can be easily removed if the landlord wants you to remove them.

d) Window coverings

Window coverings, like blinds and curtains, are used to block the view of your apartment, but they can also serve a second purpose of being an extra layer of security. For example, a landlord or building manager may take down your curtains to monitor your unit more effectively. It is best to allow people into the unit with the landlord or building management team through proper channels (such as buzzer access). This will make it much more difficult for someone to try and break in if you do not want them to.

e) Door cameras and locks

These are installed on doors, windows, and other entry points into the unit. They will prevent people from entering without authorization or if the unit is secured. This is a great way to secure your unit or prevent unwanted visitors or guests from entering that you do not want in there. They are also straightforward to install and can be done by most residential locksmiths.

f) Power control boxes

These are used in multi-unit buildings to grant access to certain tenants while denying others. It is generally easier to grant a tenant access before moving in, so if you do not want a tenant to be given access right away, this will make it more difficult for them.

g) Home control systems

These systems allow the most significant advantage of monitoring and controlling each unit from one central location. They are often used for security purposes and can include the ability of tenants who are authorized by the landlord or building management team to monitor, change or disarm their system.

How to manage the management companies

Managing management companies is an essential part of real estate investing. This is a big responsibility; it takes commitment and skill to do well.

It's important to understand that all kinds of management companies exist. The three most common types are:

a) Full-service management.

This is the most common type of management that real estate investors use. Whereas FSMs do everything for you, semi-autonomous ('Se') managers can work alongside you to manage your deals or be completely independent and run their deals independently.

b) Semi-autonomous managers.

These are the 'middle ways' between FSMs and fully autonomous managers.

- The FSM acts as a contract director, while the Se manager has the role of managing agent.
- The FSM acts as a project manager and developer, while the Se manager provides independent management services to investors on a portion of your deals.
- The Se manager provides complete management services on 50% or more of your deals. If you use this type, you will want to note precisely what percentage each one will be working for each deal and set clear boundaries in contracts based on their preferred percentage (50%, 75%, etc.).

c) Fully autonomous managers.

They are entirely independent of you as the investor and have their deals parallel yours. They may have staff who work directly for them or use contractors (freelancers). Whatever the situation, it is essential to ensure you agree on things before they start.

Here are some tips to help you manage them effectively:

a) Don't try and micromanage: You need to get out of their way when they are running their deals and stop worrying so much about their actions. Many real estate investors have difficulty letting go of control, but this is essential if they are going to be successful managers that result in consistent profits for their portfolios. However, you need to keep an eye on their activities and review them at least once a year to ensure they are doing a good job.

b) Match the right manager with the right type of deal: This seems obvious, but it's essential. You wouldn't put a construction manager in charge of a rehab project or an independent manager in charge of an existing property.

As an investor, you need to hire the right company for each job if you want to be successful. You wouldn't want to put an FSM in charge of a hotel, an FSM in charge of a condo, or an FSM in charge of retail units. For long-term success, you want to match each one with the right type of deal that they can manage well. Some companies will do better on some deals than others, so you may need to evaluate all your options to find the proper match and then try to get the best deal possible.

c) Invest in a good portfolio: Not only will carefully selecting the right manager help you make more money over time, but it will also reduce risk and help your manager grow as quickly as possible. It is essential to look at a company's track record and the experience of its staff to ensure they are the right match for your portfolio. Make sure each team has an entire team of experienced staff who have had success with similar projects.

d) Have regular meetings: This may seem like a boring part, but it helps manage each one as well as your deals and ensures progress is being made. If you don't meet regularly with your management companies, then it's easy for things to fall through the cracks and not get done to your satisfaction. It's essential to set up regular meetings at least once per month and ensure they are all attended by the majority of your team. They will find it frustrating if they are meeting as a group, but you are unaware they exist. Make sure you participate in each and have an opportunity to review their progress and offer guidance on improving operations.

Buying materials or should the builder?
When it comes to buying materials, you have three options:

a) Buying materials yourself

This is when you buy the materials but outsource the construction to a builder and then purchase the completed house.

b) Hiring a builder

This is when you hire a builder and then purchase any materials that are needed for them to complete your home.

c) Choosing from pre-built homes

This is when you buy materials like flooring, lighting accents, and appliances from suppliers who sell them at wholesale prices (usually). Then you order the house from one of their contractors, who will assemble it on-site. Once you finish this process, you'll have a completed home with no work required!

Knowing which option is best for any individual is not always easy because it depends on personal preferences and goals.

So how do you know when it is a good idea to get material from suppliers rather than buy it yourself? Well, it all depends on your situation.

One of the best things about getting materials this way is that you can typically get them at a lower price than you'd find while buying them yourself. This is because they're wholesale prices and usually purchased in bulk. And when you can purchase materials in bulk at a low price, you have the opportunity to save money.

When buying materials yourself, you save money because you don't have much overhead. However, this is also an ideal scenario for people who want to learn about construction and real estate investing. While you spend more on labor and materials upfront (and during construction), you'll better understand the entire process and experience since you're purchasing these things yourself.

When hiring a builder, you'll be able to finish your home faster because they'll do all the work for you. But as with most things in life, this comes with a price. And in this case, that means that you'll need to pay the builder and their labor costs during construction.

Regarding materials from suppliers, they allow you to get your home done faster. However, you may also face more issues during construction if you're unaware of the various details of building a home like this.

And when it comes to building yourself, some things only come from experiences, such as substandard materials and poor-quality craft. But unless you're highly knowledgeable in construction and real estate investing, you might have to hire more help than if you had chosen to buy materials from a supplier.

When it comes to building a house or what type of experience you want, this is one of the many decisions that will influence whether or not your home will be worth more in the future. This is why it makes sense that learning as much as possible about these issues as early on in the process is ideal.

One way to experiment with different options is to determine how much money you need to spend on materials and labor. This way, you'll have a better idea of your upfront costs.

And since you have a good idea of how much the project will cost, you can decide whether you need to hire some help.

Of course, one of the best ways to get started is by finding out what others are doing to get started on their own. You can visit local meetings, find people online who build homes in your area, or even find posts on social media sites like Facebook and Instagram about people working on projects. The opportunity is likely out there if you're focused enough and willing to put in the time and effort needed to find it!

What to ask for when a builder completes a job

When a builder completes a job, you should ask for the following:

a. a copy of the completed building plan in case you need to apply for permits or building inspection.
b. a certificate from the local municipality that has been issued following the Building Regulation 2013, identifying who constructed and inspected the work.
c. a certificate of completion for any electrical or plumbing work and a receipt for any compensation paid.
d. a statement from your builder's (or real estate agent's) insurance company if they provide indemnity cover.
e. a copy of the building code enforcement verification as issued by the local municipality, if this is required. Commonly called a Building Code Compliance Verification
f. a receipt for any damages incurred.
g. a certificate from your homeowner insurance company (or mortgage servicer) if they are providing indemnity cover; and
h. a certificate of completion from your local real estate broker if they will receive commissions on resale or rental income. On completion of the house, it is important to ask that you obtain a receipt for all monies paid out.
i. a copy of the rental agreement, if applicable.
j. a replacement grant-in-lieu section 1 notice from the local council should your existing house be demolished and replaced with a new house. You will not be issued a new Section 1 Notice if your new house is structurally the same as your existing building.

Suppose a builder has completed the work, and you do not ask for the above items. This helps if you need to apply for building permits and inspections. In that case, it means that if your house were demolished or extensively destroyed by fire (in which case a new house will be required), you would not be able to claim compensation from the standard insurance policy of the builder/real estate agent (because your request for compensation will have been denied).

Keep up to date with local regulations, e.g., sign up for newsletters
As a long-distance investor, you must keep up to date with the local regulations. This is because you may not live in the area, and you stand to lose out if the market drops and you have a property there.

Sign up for newsletters to keep updated with local laws that affect your investment. If anything changes, you will know about it before it affects your long-distance real estate investments. As a long-distance investor, this helps you make informed decisions about when and what to buy.

If you are not living in the area you are investing in, it is a good idea to keep up to date with how the local conditions are changing. For example, if you are investing in a town experiencing an increase in crime rates, you should know this before investing there.

This way, you won't end up blocked out of your investment. This is because your property will be more attractive to potential buyers if the local area is safe.

By keeping up to date with local laws and conditions, you can effectively avoid missing out on a property investment because the market has changed. So if your investment property is affected by a drop in its value, you will know this before investing. In this way, you can make long-distance real estate investments a success. And gain lasting wealth as a result.

There are various types of local regulations that may affect your investment. These include:

a) Crime rates

As a long-distance investor, you must keep up to date with crime rates. This is because when you buy a property, you trust your future income and safety on the property. It can be pretty painful when this is taken away from you.

So, if you are investing in a property in an area with high crime rates, you may want to reconsider this. This is because your property will be less attractive to potential buyers. And so you may end up selling at a loss.

For example, if your property were in a town with regular carjackings, you would want to reconsider investing there. This is because potential buyers would hate the thought of living in that environment and so they will not buy the property.

b) Property taxes

Property taxes are a tax that the owner of the property pays. It is usually paid monthly and covers the cost of utilities, streets, lights, schools, etc. In short, it covers basic essential services for the local community.

For example, if you invest in a property located in an area with high taxes, this can have a detrimental effect on your investment because you may have to pay more each month to cover these costs and your interest payments.

So, if you are someone whose income is not very large, then this may mean that you need to sacrifice the ability to live in a particular area for investment.

c)Reputation and attitude of locals

There is a great deal of local knowledge that surrounds an area. And this can be used to your advantage when making long-distance real estate investments. For example, if you invest in a property located in a town where the locals are very welcoming, this will make potential buyers want to buy your property.

On the other hand, if the locals are unfriendly, this could make potential buyers not want to buy your property.

So, as a long-distance investor, you need to keep an eye on how the locals feel in an area. And use this knowledge to make sure that you have made a successful investment in a safe location.

d) Properties that are affected by natural disasters

Some areas have a higher risk of natural disasters. This is because flooding and droughts are more common in certain areas. So if you are investing in an area with a high risk, you need to be aware of this before making your purchase.

For example, if you are buying a property in an area with a high risk of flooding, you must ensure that the property is insured. This way, your investment can be protected against such things as floods.

So, as a long-distance investor, you need to be aware of the natural disasters and hazards that might affect your investment. Otherwise, you could lose thousands of dollars because flooding washes away your home or a drought dries out your crops.

When considering local regulations, it is much easier to avoid missing out on a property investment because of local conditions. This is because you have the knowledge needed to make long-distance real estate investments a success and gain lasting wealth.

Chapter 7: Types of Investment Strategies for Long Distance

Investment strategies for long-distance investors are different because they require investors to know more about the markets and connections before making purchases.

The following are the types of investment strategies:

a) Investing off the plan:

Off-the-plan investments are a risky investment strategy that should only be performed by an experienced investor with knowledge of the real estate market.

The main advantage of investing off the plan is that it allows investors to gain exposure to specific markets without the costs and risks associated with buying property. In terms of long-distance, off-the-plan investments are most applicable to investors from Europe who live in North America and wish to invest in cities such as Vancouver, Toronto, Calgary, or Montreal.

In general, investing in plans is a good way for investors to enter a market before it becomes popular. For example, Vancouver has experienced much growth in the past decade, and investors who have invested in the city during this time have made significant profits.

The main downside of investing in the plan is that it can be an expensive and risky strategy. Most plan investments offer "no inspection, no cancellation"; if investors are not satisfied with the development, they cannot cancel their investment. There is also a risk of overpaying for the property if the price of the property is set high. It is also important to remember that not all off-the-plan investments are profitable, as many developers fail to complete their projects; this means investors will be left with nothing.

b) Investing in distressed properties: In most countries, it's easy to find a distressed property investor who will buy your home at a discount by purchasing your mortgage note or equity in your property. Mortgage notes are an asset purchased after a homeowner defaults on their loan. This allows you to sell your property to a distressed property investor without having your home listed for sale.

Typically, this is not the most significant investment because there are a lot of risks. Some risks include foreclosure, paying off foreclosures, investor failure, and fraud. Foreclosure means the homeowner is three months behind on their mortgage payments. If a foreclosure occurs, the bank will take ownership of the house. It is important to note that in many cases, investors can purchase houses at a discount if they buy a mortgage note, but they will still lose money if they buy the house when it goes into foreclosure. This can cost investors thousands of dollars in lost equity and raise cash to purchase the property. Investors have to expect that "the grass is always greener" and that their investment in the property will not provide them with an exceptional return.

c) Buying a property before it is built: This is a strategy that most long-distance investors undertake because it allows them to buy or sell the property at a time when they have the "ultimate control." The disadvantage of this strategy is that it may be more expensive than purchasing properties as they are being built, but the upside is that you can make a profit on your investment.

When an investor buys real estate before it is built, they are purchasing the land and what it will potentially be worth once the property is constructed. The long-distance investor can build a property they want, and the variables are limitless. They can decide how big they want to make the property, what kind of house they wish to live in, or how many rooms they want to allocate for rental units. Investors can decide if they want to build a hotel, condo, or apartment building. These variables may significantly impact an investor's investment and property value.

Investors who buy before it is built can do whatever they want with their property. Some investors can decide to build a house on a large piece of land and sell it at market value.

Look for properties run down and fix them up

Looking for a property run down and fixing it up means you must spend time looking for properties in disrepair. If you find a property and believe the price is attractive, you should schedule a time to see what needs doing and how much it will cost. Of course, there are a lot of factors at play here, and it might not always be possible for you to buy the property when first found.

This might mean you have to consider a second-hand property that you can start with. In this scenario, expect to pay more than you would for a new property, and there's also the chance it may not meet your needs in the long term.

However, buying a second-hand property and then spending the time, money, and energy on getting it up to scratch is likely to increase your chances of making a better return than investing in new properties.

Running a property from a distance can be difficult, so we have created the following guide to help you get started. This is for those looking at taking a property that needs fixing up or that requires being cleaned up and then working from there.

You might buy a little further away from the city than you'd like, but it will be much cheaper. To do this, you need to be organized and get used to working with contractors in other areas.

You should also assess how much time will be spent looking for properties and consider whether or not this is suitable for your circumstances. The more time you can spend, the better your chances of making money overall, but it might take up too much of your schedule if you are tied to other commitments.

This is a commitment, so if you invest in long-distance real estate investing, ensure you are ready for the task.

When it comes to long-distance investing, people often need the money faster than they can find a property. That's because working remotely or from another continent can often be expensive. Sure, if you are on a budget, it may be possible to buy overseas, but with some severe organizing and planning, you might discover that it is possible to get around that.

Run-down properties can be cheaper than you think. A property that is run down may be in desperate need of work, but there's a chance this could mean that it is cheaper to buy than something that's already been refurbished.

You can spend too much on a property as a result, as you'll want to know that the funds are in place before purchasing. If you are buying from overseas, getting the funds out and into your account might take longer. This means risk is associated with spending large amounts of money before getting the cash in hand.

Buying run-down properties require a lot of patience and severe research skills. Getting a property up to scratch can take time, which you must consider when considering investments from a distance. It could be that there are less-than-ideal situations where you have the funds available, but the property isn't ready to be sold yet.

This means that you might make an investment but not have the property available for sale for 30 or 40 days, which is something that your investors aren't going to like. Should this happen regularly, it is likely to get a little tiresome, too, as people start asking questions about what's happening with their money.

How to systemize short-term lets for long-distance landlords

Long-distance real estate investing is quickly becoming a popular way of making money. Unlike other types of investments, long-distance investing has one significant advantage: it can be conducted in the short term. Many people who do this don't plan on buying a property for themselves and instead try to find great deals for quick rentals. If you want to get into the game and do it right, follow these simple steps as a guideline when looking for properties and let them take care of finding renters from there!

The idea behind long-distance real estate investing is that landlords spend years negotiating a good deal with investors before finally selling their property at an acceptable price. Some will have a nightmare signing paperwork, making it hard to manage their properties effectively.

They can be able to systemize short term lets by:

a. Find property management companies that can help you manage your property. You would want to get the best rates possible at this stage.
b. Consider the people moving into your property and whether they will stay for a long time or just a few months.
c. When you are looking for property, look for ones that are cheap enough to ensure that you get back more than what you pay for rent from it in the first few months and years of investment.
d. It would help if you also looked for specific neighborhoods with good reputations and lots of people who would move in and stay for extended periods.
e. You can also find opportunities by searching on real estate websites where you post your particulars if anyone is looking to rent their properties out.

You can also rent out rooms in your home if you still live there and have an extra room or two that you aren't using. This is an excellent way to make extra cash when you visit your hometown and supplement the money you earn from being a long-distance landlord.

How to systemize House of Multiple Occupation

House of Multiple Occupation is a long-term wealth-building strategy, especially for real estate investors. It's a business model that provides income without a substantial up-front investment. It's a system that you can only get better at.

It's not a "trendy" or "in-demand" market, but it will continue to work because people need to live, no matter what. And the world will always be full of students (enrolled or not), young professionals, and working-class people who want to live in the city center but cannot afford it on their own.

You can systemize the House of Multiple Occupation by:

a. Selecting the right project at the correct location. You will compete with other investors for this property type and need to know precisely what you're looking for. Don't get lost in the hype—stick to your plan, develop a business model and stick to it.
b. Find suitable tenants to rent rooms in your House of Multiple Occupation setup. And not just any tenants but the right ones. Tenants who are reliable and can pay their rent on time (and eventually help you generate more income) are the key.
c. Securing a lease and getting tenants to sign it. You need tenants that will pay their rent on time—without having any problems with the landlord or management staff. It would help if you found tenants that will stick with you for a long time (long-term lease).
d. Finding a good property manager/property management company that will help you manage the place (and also help you capture value when you're ready to sell your rental units.).
e. Keeping track of your rental income. As you grow, you will start small, and so will your property management company. When the time comes to sell, charge a premium because you have strong-running business models with proven records.

Joint ventures

Joint ventures are said to be the most profitable real estate investments. This is so because the partners share the responsibility, risks, and rewards equally. For joint ventures to be successful, be sure to have a great partnership with your partner. Be sure you have the same goals and time constraints regarding real estate investments. This means you have to have the same timeline in which you want to sell your investment for the profits to be split fairly.

Another important thing is that you can use a Joint venture agreement. This will help keep track of everything between both parties, so there are no issues regarding dividing the profits. Most of all, be sure that you and your partner can get along well and that you are on the same page regarding goals.

If you approach them correctly, joint venture partnerships can benefit both parties.

A great benefit of a joint venture partnership is that the money is not entirely coming from your pocket. In addition to using another's capital, by splitting profits, you can use their money for repairs or investment necessities. This way, the risk will not be as high for both parties involved.

The disadvantages of joint ventures are that real estate is constantly changing, and there is no guarantee that you will see any return on investment with a partner. Another problem is that the agreement can become challenging to maintain. Sometimes, a joint venture can be set up so that there is a lot of stress and friction between the partners.

The best way to approach a joint venture is by ensuring that you and your partner have similar goals. Doing this will make it easy for you to make decisions regarding purchasing real estate investments on behalf of your partner.

Joint ventures are not always necessary but essential to real estate investing. If you are considering joining forces with another investor, or if you know someone getting started in real estate investing, it might be a good idea to try out this investment with them.

Chapter 8: Tips on How to Become a Successful Long-Distance Landlord

For you to become a successful long-distance landlord, here are some tips you should consider:

a) have reliable tenants

Your property will automatically become a good investment when you have reliable tenants. You have to give them a big room(I think about $200m^2$), a reasonable price and good property maintenance.

b) have a trusted agent

Because you are a long-distance landlord, you can't see your house from time to time. So, it would help if you had a reliable agent who could manage everything. If the agent is dishonest, they might be charged for it by the authorities. (you might lose your deposit)

c) keep in touch with your tenants and be an understanding landlord

When your tenant moves out, please do not smoke in front of them or behave rudely because they don't like it. Also, don't take away all your furniture, appliances, or anything valuable (if they are yours) because they might want to stay there for a long time.

d) don't overpay

Don't overpay your property; make it just enough to get good tenants. Better to invest little and wait three years than invest too much and leave a bad taste in your mouth in just one year. It's better to do it this way because waiting will save your deposit if the tenant leaves without paying you any month's rent.

e) make sure that the house is lovely, and you have spent some money inside.

f) don't be greedy

You might have a good tenant but want to increase the rent. You might say that they are too cheap and you can't live off the amount of rent they are paying. It will help if you think twice before you do this, as that won't benefit you in any way in the future. You might lose your house, with all your furniture and everything. It's better to take what you can get because it's a matter of money, not pride.

g) don't live beyond your financial limits

You have to spend your money wisely. If you are not in a position to be able to pay off the mortgage, then you might find long-term tenants who will stay in their houses for an extended period and get good profits. You have to be wise enough and adjust your income accordingly because one day, you may lose everything because of your wrong choice.

Should you partner with a local investor?

Partnering with a local investor can be the best way to gain the knowledge, network, and connections necessary to build a thriving real estate investing business. Local investors will have insight that you can't find on the internet, and they'll offer invaluable guidance along the way.

Some investors have an exclusive agreement with a local buyer when selling their property. And if they don't currently have one lined up, they may know someone interested in your property specifically because it's in an area of high demand. Partnering with a local investor also helps protect you from buyer's remorse when you find out about things like zoning restrictions or covenants after signing the dotted line.

Because they're local, they have more control over the situation than you do. The biggest problem with partnering with a local investor is that you may be unable to do the deal without them. And if your deal falls through, you may get stuck with a piece of property that you didn't want to be involved with in the first place.

If you decide to partner with a local investor, ensure you're familiar with their real estate investing philosophy. If they're looking for a long-term investment, they may focus on repairing the home or developing it into an income-producing property. A local investor looking to cash in on an investment could be willing to sell out quickly, even if the deal isn't exactly what you had in mind.

Growing population

A growing population means an increased demand for housing. With more people to house, you can bet that property values will go up too. This is good news for a real estate investor because it means higher rental values and potential profit margins. More people means an increased demand for real estate, which translates to an increased potential for capital growth.

An increase in population is one of the reasons that houses are getting more expensive. The other reason is because of inflation. As the cost of living goes up, people who have to put food on their tables need to get a job that pays more to keep up with rising prices.

Because more and more people are bringing in a paycheck, it is hard for the average person to save money these days. A mortgage is expensive and complicated to afford if you don't have a four-year degree and comprehensive health insurance. In other words, it's just not worth it for many working-class people. Instead, they're going out and buying houses for as much money as humanly possible.

Real estate investing has always been an expensive hobby, but now it's getting more expensive due to the increasing demand for houses. The house of the future will be built to be smaller and more compact, but it will cost a fortune. Because of this, we will all be able to buy fewer houses for our money as time goes on.

Increased demand for housing means more people can afford to buy various types of homes. That means that there will be more demand for new construction as well as for renovations and remodels. Perhaps this is a good thing, or maybe not; time will tell. Either way, there will be more jobs for architects, builders, electricians, and plumbers.

Age distribution

Age distribution has a significant impact on the housing market. Older people tend to live closer to their children and grandchildren. As a result, they purchase less-exotic homes in more affordable areas than younger groups because they need more space. Generation X and Baby Boomers are now looking for rental property as they age, while Millennials are deciding whether or not to buy property at all because of their preference to work instead of living in a particular city. This shifts the burden onto Millennial renters when it comes time for them to move into their own homes. Real estate investors should realize that specific housing markets are more appealing to older generations of people and target more affordable homes in these areas.

Contrary to the above, with more families staying together for the long term, there will be an increase in demand for larger homes because of the addition of children, grandchildren, or older parents. The ability to move out and buy a separate property will become less practical as it is more important that all family members stay together. This trend, previously discussed in the context of demographic changes and "empty nest," will cause an increase in demand for larger homes and a decreased demand for smaller ones because of the desire to live together.

Stable employment

When an individual has stable employment, this increases the likelihood of long-term wealth. This is a result of two factors:

a. stable employment increases the amount of income an individual has,
b. it provides a sense of security and stability. Sadly, many individuals don't have stable employment, which creates issues in figuring out how to invest money in a way that would lead to increased wealth.

Here are some essential points to note about stable employment:

a. If a person does not have a stable job, saving money for future needs and investing will be difficult. This can lead to a situation where there is no money for investment because it is being spent on current needs, which include necessities and financial obligations such as mortgages, car loans, etc.

b. Stable employment also means that individuals invest their money in safe assets such as savings and retirement plans. Part of that is due to stable employment, but it depends on the individual's knowledge about the financial markets and how best he can afford to invest his money.
c. If individuals with stable jobs learn about the alternatives to savings and retirement, they tend to increase their wealth due to education and accessibility.
d. If stable employment leads an individual to invest in savings and retirement plans, the individual misses out on the wealth-building opportunities of direct real estate investment. This is because these plans do not provide enough yield.

If an individual has stable employment, he can save money for future needs like retirement. Still, it will be less likely that he will invest it in other forms of investment like real estate, which could lead to a higher return on investment and, thus, more incredible wealth over time.

Schools

Schools also contribute to real estate investing; this is seen through programs that teach students about the business of real estate investing. Some programs have even created specializations in real estate investing so that students can get an even deeper understanding of this field. When students graduate from these programs, they are well-versed in the skills for becoming successful real estate investors.

Students can learn through their schools about the history of real estate investing and the process of finding and negotiating with property owners to buy their homes. Once a student finds a property they want to purchase, they must find a way of obtaining financing for this purchase. Loans from banks that do not require collateral are usually the easiest way for students to obtain financing for real estate investments. These types of loans are common because banks know that it is unlikely that students will default on their loan obligations. Students must create their venture capital to make an even larger purchase. This is known as purchasing an investment property (commonly referred to as cash flow properties) with an individual's capital.

Students interested in going into business for themselves can even help start up a new real estate investment firm through their school. This is known as incubating a business. This could be done on the school's campus or in another area that a student has been able to secure. Another step that some schools are taking to promote real estate investment is partnering with industry firms so that students can gain practical knowledge of how this field works while still attending classes on campus.

Crime

Investing in areas where crime rates are higher can be a good idea, even if you don't expect to make money from it.

Real estate investing is a volatile business, and anyone who has invested in the past will tell you that it is essential to invest with your eyes open: understanding your risk tolerance and knowing what to expect. It's also important to remember that crime rates on the side of your investments could end up causing losses because of the effect they could have on your investments.

When you start, you shouldn't expect to get rich overnight. It's good to know that crime rate-wise, the area where you would invest will not be one of the worst ones. You can choose to invest even in areas with higher risk and lower returns as long as you know what kind of risk it is and what kind of return you can expect. If a cheap property in an area with a high crime rate would give you a low guaranteed return, then that's your choice: you should invest in an area with higher returns and a higher crime rate if you're willing to take that risk.

Crime rates can also be affected by your property, and some investor strategies can significantly affect crime rates. For example, getting a high return from your rental property could attract more criminals to the area as they look for places to commit crimes. This might cause your property to suffer from more break-ins, but that would still mean a higher return on your investment.

It's always important to know the introductory crime rate of the area, but if you are planning to invest in an area with a high crime rate, it's also a good idea to know what kind of crime would affect you.

Vacancy rate

One of the best ways to find an excellent long-term investment is to look closely at the vacancy rate of the area you're interested in. A low vacancy rate means you'll likely be able to rent and then sell the property at a higher price later. A high vacancy rate, on the other hand, can mean a few things. No properties are available for sale in that area, or it's just undervalued due to demand (or lack thereof) that you can buy it for next-to-nothing and move on to your next target with a minimal investment loss. The key here is realizing which type of market you're investing in. You'll want to buy in the right market if you see sustainable income from your investments.

A higher vacancy rate, especially in an area with a large population of retirees or small families, is not necessarily alarming. Because many houses are available for sale, people will visit your office frequently looking to rent your commercial spaces. This can mean that the demand for housing is much lower in the area, but the demand for commercial space, owned and managed by you, is much higher. It's important to note that commercial properties can also see vacancy rates, so you'll want to keep an eye on your total property value and compare the actual income it generates to the price you bought the property for. This will help you to determine if you're actually making money or just spending lots of time managing a space that isn't worth much.

What to Delegate

Knowing what to delegate is a critical success factor for any remote investor. Some tasks, if delegated correctly, will save the time and energy of the investor and result in a lower acquisition cost. These tasks can be delegated to an employee or outsourced to a third-party vendor.

Here are a few things that are extremely helpful to delegate:

a) Lead Generation – You can hire employees or vendors who know how to prospect for leads and follow up with potential investors. Most people don't like selling anyway, so delegating this task will save you time and allow you to focus on the essential aspects of your business, such as finding deals, negotiating terms, and managing the investors after closing escrow.

b) Property Management – While you may not want to delegate complete management of the property, most investors are paying property managers $500-$2500 per month to run their rental properties. That's a lot of money for something that you can probably do yourself. If you opt to do this, focus on the accounting aspect of the management rather than physically managing the property.

c) Bookkeeping and Accounting – Most investors struggle with these areas. Outsourcing these tasks will save you a lot of time and money if your weak area is accounting and bookkeeping.

d) Legal – You can have lawyers draft your letters, agreements, and other documents for a fraction of what law firms charge their clients.

What to Automate

Automating your real estate investing can help you save time, minimize risks and build a passive income. Automated investing may seem scary to some people, but it doesn't have to be. There are many great ways to automate real estate investing while maintaining control of your portfolio. These ways include:

a) Investing for multiple properties.

This means you must find a way to source good deals, research, and make offers before your competition. You'll also be able to find properties in multiple locations. This will eliminate competition and allow you to buy with cash in a shorter time and keep your money working longer if you invest in an investment property.

b) Investing in more properties.

This is easier said than done, but it can be automated easily with suitable systems, procedures, and mindset. It will require you to manage multiple deals simultaneously, which may seem overwhelming, but it isn't if you use the right processes.

c) Maximising deals.

You can use the same strategies for finding deals, making offers, and building rapport with real estate agents. Streamlining these processes will give more time for due diligence and analysis of the market. This will lead to more investments with higher returns over an extended period. This will allow you to make better investment decisions resulting in tremendous success.

d) Marketing your services.

One of the most critical aspects of this business is marketing your services. You need to reach out to a large audience and attract their attention. The more people you can attract, the more deals you'll have.

e) Buying for fun and profit.

You must have fun when investing in real estate. If financial freedom is your goal, then it can be achieved by following these five strategies for automating your real estate investing.

f) Property management/property manager

Automating this process can also free up a lot of time you could otherwise use for investments, networking, or other essential things.

g) Saving time.

Automating your real estate investing can save you a lot of time. It will allow you to focus on finding deals, managing your portfolio, and growing your business. This can all be done without worrying about the mundane tasks that come with property management.

h) Building a passive income stream.

Passive income is like a money machine that keeps working for you even when you are sleeping or on vacation. This type of income is necessary because it will give you choices in life and more financial options when it comes to buying properties, saving for retirement, and using money as an investment vehicle rather than a commodity for survival.

What to Eliminate and Prevent

There are several things that you have to eliminate and prevent to become a successful long-distance investor; they are:

a) the idea of making a quick buck by buying and flipping properties.

This means that you cannot afford not to make any money because if you don't, then it's not worth your time.

b) the notion that you have to quit your job to be a successful investor.

This means you're in it for the long haul since quitting your job will only cause stress, and you'll become impulsive when making decisions.

c) the idea of getting rich quickly.

There is no reason for you to rush into anything or take unnecessary risks – there is always a better deal around the corner.

d) getting emotionally involved with real estate. It will help if you stay objective and professional. Otherwise, things can turn out very badly in the end.

e) being scared that you'll get ripped off.

This means you're either new to real estate investing or don't have the right tools or knowledge to make suitable investments.

f) not understanding the risks and advantages of real estate investing.

You need to know what's at stake before jumping in. Otherwise, you stand the chance of losing your money and credibility.

g) thinking that "real estate is for rich people."

Pretty self-explanatory. The possibilities are endless, and you can reach the top even if you were born poor. This means that there is no reason why you cannot be part of it if you so desire.

h) thinking you're too young or old to be a successful investor.

This is not true since many investors started young, and in some cases starting later in life is better since it gives you more experience and business acumen.

Conclusion

Long-distance real estate investing is a viable option for retirees and those with stable incomes. It can be more challenging to appraise properties and becomes more costly when you factor in travel, but the payoffs are worthwhile. It's worth comparing your financial situation against the expenses of local investments and what it would cost you to move. Ultimately, long-distance investing might not be suitable for everyone. There's no such thing as the size fits all regarding your wealth management.

It's best if you start by examining your situation before moving forward with long-distance real estate investment plans. Consider your goals, the amount of time you have, and how much you spend traveling. Talk to your spouse or family about their plans and concerns. The fact is that long-distance investing can be a complex undertaking and requires more than just travel expenses, but it does offer significant benefits for those who are invested in it.

Investors interested in traveling for their investments can seriously benefit from long-distance real estate investing. However, you should ensure a stable income and the financial means to invest in multiple properties.

Long-distance real estate investing is a field that many investors want to venture into, but it's essential that you know what you're getting into and if it's suitable for your situation. If you're planning on pursuing long-distance investing, then make sure that your area of expertise is one where workers are in high demand. If not, then find an investor who specializes in these areas so they can help you with the rest of the process and hire someone local to get the inspections done when needed. You never want to be put in a position where you're losing money, and that's why having a partner can make your return on investment much more substantial.

Also, suppose you do end up investing in properties that are located in a different state or country. In that case, you can always talk to your mortgage broker or contact someone who works with international investments. These investors might be able to help you access different types of financing for these types of properties. Most investors agree that long-distance real estate investing is worth it if the numbers add up.

Long-distance investing might be what you need if you're struggling with your finances or have a ton of stress in your life. Some risks are associated with long-distance investing, but the rewards are there for those who are patient enough to wait for the right deal. You can also learn from other investors in these remote locations when getting financing or finding an investor. Make sure you take care of yourself and don't go into this investment blindly just because another one is promising more money faster.

Many investors compare long-distance real estate investing to local investing because both involve preparing properties that can be sold at a profit. In terms of accessibility, they're almost identical, but some aspects make them different as well. For instance, long-distance real estate investing requires you to research the market, find a property that can earn money, and hire someone local to take care of the necessary inspections.

There's also a time difference that comes into play with long-distance investing. The work you do during office hours will be "lost time" for local investors; every hour and day that passes without action is another hour wasted.

All in all, long-distance investing is within reach for those with sound real estate investment experience and the ability to handle property management from afar. People interested in this investment type should keep several things in mind before they begin searching for properties.

They should have a solid understanding of the market they're targeting. The location, the outlook, and the demand for that particular area are all essential factors when making a profitable investment.

They also need to be able to find properties that will bring in enough money so they can afford to make repairs and produce a profit. At the same time, though, they have to consider the cost of travel time and loss of income involved with being far away from their marketplace.

Investment strategies vary depending on the real estate market. For example, if they're looking to make a long-term investment, their best bet would be to look for properties that will bring in a steady cash flow over time and are also repairable.

If you have reservations about traveling long distances, you can always consider buying some pieces of property on the internet or by phone because these can be sold and shipped to your doorstep. It would help if you also tried to learn about local real estate investing in your area to supplement what you do from the other side of the country or world.

Those interested in long-distance investing should start by outlining their goals and budgeting any expenses they may have. Next, they must consider what kind of real estate investment fund they'll need. Will it be a bond fund or a property pool? By understanding the strategies these organizations offer, investors can make suitable investments in their future. However, buying these types of funds can require a lot of research and time, so investors need to be able to afford that much time before they get started with their new venture.

Long-distance investing is something that many people want to pursue, but you must look at your situation when making this investment decision. If you're interested in long-distance investing, ensure your area of expertise is one where workers are in high demand. If not, then find an investor who specializes in these areas so they can help you with the rest of the process and hire someone local to get the inspections done when needed.

www.ingramcontent.com/pod-product-compliance
Lightning Source LLC
Chambersburg PA
CBHW052344220526
45465CB00003BA/947